MW00936941

the sea gypsy philosopher

To Bill,

Bravo on your visionary work!
So few realize that there
is everlasting and vital
wisdom in the "old ways."

Ray
nov 2015

The Sea Gypsy
Philosopher

Uncommon Essays
from a Thoughtful Wanderer

Ray Jason

CLUB
ORLOV
PRESS

The Sea Gypsy Philosopher:
Uncommon Essays
from a Thoughtful Wanderer

© 2015 Ray Jason

Publication date: May 1, 2015

ISBN-13: 978-1511976954
ISBN-10: 1511976950

Cover photo: Dmitry Orlov
Author's portrait: Fred Evans

Club Orlov Press
http://ClubOrlovPress.blogspot.com
cluborlovpress@gmail.com

Introduction

M Y FRIEND Ray calls himself a philosopher, but he is more accurately described as an artist. As you'll discover, he has achieved remarkable artistry in juggling knives, torches and bowling balls; I hope that you'll also enjoy Ray's gifts as a prose artist and a poet in the pages that follow. More significantly, he has perfected the art of living, reducing his physical requirements and thus his budget down to bare essentials, encapsulating them all in his modest but very capable sailboat. Doing so has given him the freedom to spend his days sailing around an idyllic and pristine tropical archipelago, anchoring wherever he pleases for as long as he pleases, communing with the locals both animal and human, rowing ashore to pick fruit, going for a swim, or sitting up on deck, his back against the mast, composing these essays with a clipboard and pen.

Ray was anchored next to us for some of the time we worked together on this book, and I saw for myself just how closely his deliberate, well-paced, contemplative way of living approximates the ideal of personal freedom. This freedom has given Ray the time, mental and physical space, and the perspective to focus intensely on the multitude of predicaments that beset the world, such as nuclear self-annihilation, runaway climate change and the steady morphing of the U.S. into a police state. Most people, who endlessly sail their little dinghy around the three racing buoys of work-shopping-home, have neither the time nor the mental fortitude to adequately consider such matters, never mind respond to them with anything more constructive than anxiety and compulsive shopping for "survival" goods.

But Ray has been able to formulate and execute a plan: in almost any worst-case scenario, he and his boat will be nowhere to be found—for a while—and then drift back once the dust settles. More than two decades spent living aboard and single-handing his way around the world's oceans have prepared him for just about anything. As they say, don't try this at home, but I do hope that Ray's example inspires you to try something—anything—that won't leave you treading water, waiting for a helpful shark to drop by and put you out of your misery.

It seems that a measured, well-paced life in a serene setting, combined with the option to relocate to any one of 139.7 million square miles of ocean, has given Ray the ability to handle with equanimity and poise topics that fill most of us with trepidation, and to offer you an alternative, not just for some distant future, but, if you choose it, as soon as you like. What's that alternative? It is to join Ray's Sea Gypsy Tribe and get ready to sail away from trouble. If his vision strikes you as romantic, then that's because Ray *is* a romantic, following in the footsteps of Emerson and Thoreau.

I hope that you thoroughly enjoy these most extraordinary lessons from a most extraordinary being. And I hope that they will help you move in the direction of living a life that is less ordinary. Maybe it will even inspire a few of you to accept Ray's advice, move aboard and sail off, in which case Ray and I might see you out on the water.

Dmitry Orlov
April 2015
Tierra Oscura
Archipélago de Bocas del Toro
Panamá

Contents

Arise Young Sea Gypsies

*T*HE OLD FISHERMAN was smiling as he rowed his cayuco through the twilight-tinted lagoon towards *Aventura*. As he pulled alongside, he told me in Spanish that he had some very fine fish tonight. Looking down into his bucket I agreed, and so I bought a nice fresh mangrove snapper. When I went below to get some money, I also brought back a couple of cold Balboas—the local beer. We drank them silently as we watched the sun's amber descent behind the distant volcano. Then he surprised me with an unexpected question.

"Qué país?" What country, he asked, as he pointed to the flag flying from my rigging.

"¡No país!" No country, I answered.

"¿No país?" He responded in a puzzled manner.

"Correcto, soy un gitano del mar." That's right, I am a sea gypsy.

Realizing that he still did not quite understand this, I lowered the flag down so that he could see it closely. It is an Earth Flag with the classic photo of our planet from space.

"El *mundo* es mi país. El *mar* es mi país, ¿entiendes?" The *world* is my country. The *sea* is my country. Do you understand?

1

"Si, fantástico," he said. And then we sat quietly and finished our beers as the darkening sky shadowed the bay. He passed me back the empty can and then reached into his bucket and brought out another fish. In Spanish he told me that it was a gift—"for his friend whose country is the Sea."

* * *

Ironically, the memory of this lovely episode with the ancient fisherman inspired a meditation about sailors at the opposite end of the age spectrum. The more I ponder our present world and our planetary future, the more discouraged I become. And if it is difficult for someone like me, who is sailing through his middle years, imagine how bleak it must appear for those a few decades astern of me.

And so I am writing this essay in the hopes of inspiring young people all over the world to consider adopting the sea gypsy life. I am urging them to become—as the old fisherman so eloquently expressed it—a man or woman "whose country is the Sea." And here is why...

* * *

For the last decade, the internet—and in particular the alternative media portion of it—has courageously revealed the true nature of Power in the modern world. Today, only a fool still believes that they control their own destiny via "duly elected representatives" who carry out the wishes of the people. The reality is that we do not have leaders—we have Rulers.

Plato yearned for a world of "philosopher kings" that would benevolently balance the rights of the People and the needs of the State. He would be horrified by what has actually evolved. The global leadership class (political, military, business and media) is a putrid swamp filled almost entirely with psychopaths and sociopaths. They have no concern whatsoever for the Common Good—even though they spout platitudes applauding it whenever a TV camera is nearby. They are addicts whose drug is Domination. They are money and power junkies; and they will do whatever is necessary to keep their fixes flowing. Furthermore, they are more vicious and devious than ever.

Witness the NSA spying revelations: When Edward Snowden showed the world how widespread the unlawful surveillance of practically everyone on the planet was, the reaction from the U.S. Congress should have been: "This is illegal and immoral and obscene—and it must end immediately!" But instead, they shifted the discussion to a debate over how much spying on ordinary citizens was acceptable for 'national security reasons.' So for all of the young people out there who I am trying to convince of the merits of the sea gypsy life, here is my first argument:

They Are Secretly Weaving a Total Control Web Around You.

They are tracking you through your smartphones and your computers. They are monitoring you with highway license plate readers and the GPS units in your cars. Those "smart" electric meters that they are installing are their eyes into your homes. Up in the sky above you the first drones are patrolling; and they are now admitting that over 30,000 will be launched by the end of this decade—"for your protection." And the ultimate wet dream of these control freaks is to shoot an RFID chip under your skin—providing them complete knowledge of your location and your activities. In the meantime, they will add these chips to your passports to keep track of your whereabouts.

And all of these horrible invasions of every person's right to privacy are being expanded at the same time that they are completing another phase of their control junkie plan. This is

3

my second argument in favor of abandoning the slave matrix and embracing the sea gypsy life:

They Are Militarizing The Police Not To Protect You But To Oppress You.

Those at the center of power—who I like to call The Malignant Overlords—are either aware that an economic collapse is coming or they are actually engineering that meltdown. Either way, they are mindful that a pushback from those whose lives have been destroyed is very likely. They truly understand that a torches-and-pitchforks moment may be out there on the event horizon.

And so they are arming local police departments as though they were Galactic Stormtroopers. They are now almost indistinguishable from front-line combat infantry troops. SWAT teams are multiplying like slime in a Petri dish. Tiny little towns now have military-surplus armored personnel carriers that are just one step below tanks. These in-your-face vehicles, designed to terrify and subdue the general population, are now even popping up in school districts around the country. Why does a school district need grenade launchers and semi-tanks?

So, why might The Malignant Overlords be so vigorously installing a militarized police and surveillance state? The most likely explanation is that even though they are already almost omnipotent, their lust for even more control is utterly pathological. So they seek a world where they rule and beneath them is a small group of technicians to run the surveillance and police grid. And beneath them is a massive group of modern day serfs, whose only chance to rise above serfdom is by stepping on the throats of other serfs. This leads to my third reason why the sea gypsy option is the best escape for awakened young people:

The Future They Are Offering You Is Low-Grade Serfdom

Imagine a planet that combines the worst of Aldous Huxley's *Brave New World* and George Orwell's *1984*. What you have just envisioned is *Brave New Earth 2014*. Even Orwell could not have imagined the surveillance capabilities that our contemporary Big Brother has achieved. Our rulers understand that the boot on the neck is a powerful tool of repression, but they also recognize that subtlety is even more effective. So they dazzle and distract us with electronic hypnotism that would amaze even Huxley. Almost the entire planet now walks around staring at and talking into screens. Around the clock, through hundreds of channels, the TV screams out its message of "consume and conform!" We are bombarded by a hologram-like thread of spectacle: Super Bowls, award shows, and movies that are dominated by comic book superheroes and violent special effects. And as we lap up this vapid tripe from a metastasized "un-culture," we fail to notice the profound and steady deterioration of any genuine meaning in our lives.

This is no way to live and for the young it will become even more difficult to *just live*. A college degree no longer assures a tolerable, decent-paying job. And getting that diploma usually requires taking out loans that practically make the student an indentured servant for many years after graduation. And the blue-collar work opportunities have vaporized as the obscenely greedy corporations "off-shored"—or, more accurately, *stole*—those jobs from the working class. The young are looking at a future of burger flipping, changing bedpans or being grunts in the imperial war machine.

* * *

The reason I have tried to paint such a vivid picture of the trauma that awaits the younger generation is because I have an antidote for this diseased society: Flee! More specifically, Flee to the Sea... become a man or woman "whose country is the Sea." You cannot reform the system through political action or protest or even revolt. The Malignant Overlords have it too locked down. Instead, sail away and let it collapse under the weight of its own hubris and over-reach.

While it crumbles, you can enjoy a life of authentic freedom and adventure and harmony with Nature, while surrounded by young peers who also made the same bold decision. You can reconnect with your less-domesticated and more feral self.

In one year from the moment you are reading this, you can have joined the sea gypsies already out wandering the Wide Waters. In this book there are several essays that detail exactly how to do this. Begin with the one called The Sea Gypsy Tribe and work your way through the others. For the price of just the average down payment on a house, you can own a fully-equipped, self-sufficient sailboat. But you will quickly realize that it is more than just a boat—that it is a magic carpet capable of carrying you across oceans of wonder and possibility.

* * *

I certainly realize that most of what I write often falls on deaf ears or no ears. But my "Inner Fool" keeps insisting that I strive to add a tiny bit more light to a darkening world. So I hope that one day that ancient fisherman will again row up to *Aventura* to sell me a fish. And he will be amazed to discover five or six other boats all flying the Earth Flag. Then he will think to himself: "This truly pleases my fisherman's soul—for here is an entire tribe whose country is the Sea."

The Road to the Future
Leads to the Past

*A*N ORDINARY SUNSET was about to turn extraordinary. *Aventura* was resting between voyages—way down south in the Banana Latitudes. We were anchored in a cove so serene that the birds seemed to fly at half speed in order to preserve the tranquility.

A native cayuco slowly emerged from behind one of the islands that frame this tiny bay. A man and a woman were gently rowing their dugout canoe through the pale, peach-glazed water. When they swung their bow around and faced the west, I recognized the young couple. They had stopped by yesterday and traded a freshly-caught fish for some cooking oil.

They stowed their oars in the cayuco and drifted about 30 yards off my starboard side. She leaned her back against his chest and his chin cradled the top of her head. Although the twilight panorama that we were savoring was only mediocre, I suspect that their contentment was as transcendent as mine.

Suddenly, this exquisite peacefulness was destroyed by the roar of an outboard engine as a shiny American powerboat came blasting through our little sanctuary. Two overweight guys laughed drunkenly as they watched their wake nearly capsize the little native canoe. I looked over at my neighbors and shook my head in disgust. They responded with body language that said, "Sad, sad, sad."

A few minutes later, with the euphoric spell broken, they slid a fishing line into the water, and then started to row towards a nearby island. As I watched them depart, I realized that every element of this dusk-soft panorama was so elemental, that it could have taken place 500 years ago.

While their cayuco drifted to the south, with the lovers lazily fishing, I turned back to the west and caught a glimpse of the drunken gringos roaring out of sight. Because I am blessed (or cursed) with the philosopher's need to contemplate such symbolic vignettes, I began a meditation that took me deep into the star-plush night.

-

**

Yesterday, when the couple rowed over to barter their fish, I complimented the young man on his well-crafted cayuco. With a mixture of modesty and pride he said that he had carved it himself, just as his father had taught him. And he mentioned that one of his earliest childhood memories was watching his grandfather teaching his dad his boat-shaping technique.

A single tree trunk, a few hand tools, and skill passed down the generations was all that was necessary to create this handsome cayuco that could be used for transportation, fishing or twilight romance. How simple and exquisite; and how out of step with the misnamed "real world." By contrast, the speedboat that had just annihilated the silent beauty of this little cove was a perfect symbol for our industrial-techno society.

As the Sun Sky surrendered to the Star Sky, I decided to carefully ponder the differences between these two vessels. An hour's contemplation confirmed that they are an excellent metaphor for the chasm between the primitive-tribal worldview and modern civilization. The contrasts are stark and sobering and they are a perfect illustration of the somewhat enigmatic title of this essay: "The Road to the Future Leads to the Past."

Go to any shopping mall, anywhere on the planet, and show 50 people a photo of a cayuco and a picture of a high-speed powerboat. Then ask them this simple question: "Which of these boats will become extinct in the near future?" A huge majority will respond that the little Indio canoe will soon be gone. But I firmly believe the opposite, and hopefully I can also convince you. But before examining the future of these two types of watercraft, let's consider how profoundly different they are in the present.

• **Simplicity**. The cayuco has exactly one moving part—the paddle. On the other hand, the power boat has hundreds, if not thousands—all interwoven amongst mechanical, electrical, hydraulic and electronic systems.

• **Health-promoting**. A lean, powerful human animal smoothly paddling a small boat is a universal and enduring image that can be traced back thousands and thousands of years. But an overweight, "look at me" speedboater is a phenomenon that has been around for less than a hundred years.

• **Nature-friendly**. The self-propelled cayuco allows one to blend with nature and savor it. A motorboat with its screeching outboard engine assaults nature and scares away all of the nearby neighbors of the sea and the sky.

• **Non-polluting**. The speedboat imposes its noise pollution on any creature in the vicinity, the exhaust from its engine spews poison into the air, and a longer-term form of pollution is the lack of bio-degradability of the fiberglass hull. The wooden cayuco will rot away fairly swiftly, but the powerboat will try to outlive the pyramids.

• **Personal satisfaction**. Admittedly, the owner of a gaudy new powerboat will experience some ego-stroking as he pulls into his local marina. But compare that to the pride of an Indio, who has just finished carving a cayuco. Imagine the joy he feels as he admires her sturdy but elegant lines and his delight when his excited children climb in to go for their maiden voyage.

• **Fossil-fuel freedom.** Astronomical gas prices or crippling supply interruptions are meaningless to the person in the dugout canoe. But these issues can convert that shiny pleasure boat into a money vacuum or a haunting, unused relic.

I was still contemplating fuel dependency when I heard a shout of delight from the couple in the cayuco, who were now a hundred yards down the bay. They had caught a fish. Soon they built a fire on the beach and prepared their meal with cavemen simplicity, cooking it on a stick bent over the flames. When it was ready they rotated it to let it cool. Then they enjoyed it by just pulling off delicious chunks of the fish with their fingers.

Watching this lovely couple enjoy their little feast in the same manner that their ancestors did 10,000 years ago, turned my ever-pensive mind to how much more complicated it would be for the chunky, drunken gringos to catch a fish and enjoy it for dinner. It would probably involve very expensive high-tech equipment and an underwater fish finder. As for the rustic campfire, it would be replaced by a propane barbecue grill. And this brought me back to that question that I posed earlier—"Which one of these boats is headed for extinction?" And this leads to the more significant interrogative, "Which one of these modes of living is headed for extinction?"

* * *

Most people today believe that the problems our planet faces are serious but not overwhelming. They comfort themselves by thinking that we can muddle along until some miraculous solution appears. Having carefully researched the possibility of societal collapse for many years, I vehemently disagree.

My term for the possible disasters that confront us is the Big Bad E's. This stands for Economy, Energy and Ecology. I could discuss these three meta-systems individually for hours, but it is their interconnectedness in today's society which I find most troubling. Let me focus on just one—contemporary food production, or what is normally called Big Ag. It will be obvious how intertwined and precarious every aspect of modern daily life is.

In the U.S. during the Great Depression, there were still many family farms scattered throughout the nation. So when the economic collapse hit, most of the farm children who had migrated to the big cities could return home and at least have survival food. Nowadays the overwhelming majority of agriculture is conducted on massive corporate farms, so the family farm safety valve no longer exists.

And these monolithic agribusiness tracts are entirely fossil fuel-dependent. You will not find many farmers tilling their fields behind mules or scattering manure on their soil. Every step of the modern agricultural assembly line relies on fossil fuel inputs, whether it is fuel for the tractors, combines and trucks or natural gas derivatives for the fertilizers, pesticides and insecticides.

Ecology also entwines itself negatively in Big Agriculture in both directions. As the climate crisis deepens there are more extreme weather events that destroy food production, such as severe droughts or devastating flooding. And because factory farming is so artificial and inorganic, it contributes enormously to climate destabilization. The fuel inputs in modern, large scale agriculture are so vital that some people have observed that we actually "eat oil." This may or may not be an exaggeration, but I believe that the way I phrase it is completely accurate—"Without oil, we do not eat!"

But the young couple feasting in the firelight on their just-caught fish are completely independent of modern food processing. Certainly, they sometimes go to town and buy a few staples and some treats, but if that was no longer available, they would still survive. But the hefty, drunken boaters are utterly dependent on their supermarket. This led me to assess the other basic elements of survival and how well-prepared the natives are.

However, before evaluating these differences, let me clarify my terminology. The couple that I describe in this story are what I consider Fringe Indios. Their ancestors were here long before the arrival of the white people, and due to their self-reliant capabilities, they will remain after the whites are "gone." I refer to them as "fringe" because unlike the 85 or so remaining indigenous tribes who live almost completely cut off from the modern world, these Indios exist on the fringes of it. Here's why they are so much less vulnerable to a "real world" collapse:

• **Water**. They have never been connected to any form of "the grid" whether it is electricity or piped-in water. They know which local streams are good for drinking and they know how to catch sky water.

• **Food**. Besides fishing, they also are skilled at foraging the shoreline. In the surrounding jungle they know which fruits and plants are edible. They are also skilled at primitive, low-tech cultivation. Cooking is mostly done with pots and pans over open fires.

• **Shelter**. The roofs of their homes are woven from palm trees. The only hand tools necessary for building the remainder of a house are a machete, hammer and saw. They sometimes use nails but they can also connect the timbers using twine at the joints.

• **Health**. They haven't completely lost the knowledge of which local plants are medicinal and their simple style of liv-

ing insulates them from most of the "diseases of civilization."
  • **Security**. The Indios have very little that a typical marauder would desire, which is their first line of defense. But should things become dangerous in spite of this, they can retreat to the deep jungle where most human predators would not follow.

The little campfire on the beach had now gone out, and I could hear the young couple splashing in the water. A few minutes later their play became quieter and more rhythmic. I sighed deeply, for it comforted me to realize that these lovely human animals were now pleasuring each other where the water meets the land...the same place from which our forebears had emerged so many millions of years ago.

* * *

Then my thoughts returned again to the drunken powerboaters who were probably sitting at a bar back in town laughing uproariously over how they had almost capsized "a couple of Indians" that afternoon. These so-called civilized beings are supposedly "my people." Certainly I was raised in that milieu. But miraculously, down the decades I was able to separate myself from the conventional human voyage and to view it through a different lens—from the outsider, sea gypsy perspective.

But it has been profoundly disturbing to carefully observe our species. With our enormous brains which bless us with the power of self-awareness and of language and of the arts, we could have achieved so much; but instead, we have squandered these gifts foolishly and destructively.

Rather than accepting and relishing our place in the natural order, we deceived ourselves into believing that we could rule over Nature and use it as we desired. Our hubris in this regard became so extreme that we embraced the fool's quest for infinite growth on a finite planet.

We never achieved our higher-order consciousness when it came to conflict resolution, so every century has been stained with needless blood and mutilation. We chose competition over co-operation, excess over moderation, and mindless worship of trinkets over authentic, interpersonal living. And we let our big-brain technologies seduce us. We unleashed gargantuan forces without wisely pondering the consequences, so now we are poised at the edge of the abyss. Our human intelligence and power has been so distorted and corrupted that we are on the verge of destroying our planetary support system. We are on the threshold of annihilating much of the life that exists on the one single planet amongst millions that can support life. How insane and tragic is that?

* * *

Just as my depressing ruminations began to overwhelm me, the young couple came rowing by. They nodded to me and smiled. Even though there was no moon, they glistened radiantly in the starlight. A reassuring peace came over me, for I knew that if the monstrous Leviathan of modern civilization did come tumbling down, these two lovers would survive. *They are the road to the future that leads to the past.* And perhaps on the second try, humanity will do better on that road...

A Sea Gypsy Reverie

WHAT A SWEET, sublime awakening! Three of Mother Ocean's timeless clocks gently stirred me from sleep. First, the boat shifted as the tide switched direction. Then the sun nudged just high enough to peek into one of *Aventura*'s portholes. And finally, a flock of wild parrots boisterously flew over the bay, swapping gossip and recipes.

I lay on my back wondering if the ship's geckos were smiling as joyously as me. Probably not, since they were unaware of how happily emancipated I felt. Unlike so many of my fellow humans, I was not a slave to the Tyranny of Frenzy. The Dictators of Speed and Stuff did not control me.

My plan had been to start a new essay this morning on some political or economic issue that was troubling me. But then I heard... the laughter in the mango tree. Three small cayucos were pulled up onto the beach of the little island where I was anchored. There were many tiny, one-tree islands in my neighborhood, but those all featured tall, skinny palm trees. But this one boasted an enormous mango tree. And to-day it had five giggling interlopers.

Up in the branches were two boys and a girl. They would vigorously shake the limbs trying to dislodge some of the ripe fruit. Down below a girl and a boy raced around with empty rice bags trying to catch the falling mangoes. After half an hour, the rice sacks were almost full and the kids came down from the tree. Then the five of them leaned their backs against their cayucos, stretched their bare feet into the water and savored a spring-time feast. The scene was so pure and idyllic that I could visualize Gauguin reaching for his easel and brushes.

* * *

That cinched it. There would be no meditations on serious societal problems this day. Instead, I would allow my slow, simple life in the Banana Latitudes to sweep me where it might. Feeling refreshed and energized, I decided to go for a leisurely morning swim. Before doing so, I scanned the lagoon carefully. Even here in the Archipelago of Bliss there are hazards and nuisances. But no jellyfish were visible, so I dove in enthusiastically.

My fondness for physical exercise is not motivated primarily by vanity. Certainly, I won't deny that I try to look my best, but there are other more important factors that inspire me. For one thing, it is the only health insurance that I can afford. It helps me sleep soundly and deeply. Physical exertion actually does release endorphins into your bloodstream that increase pleasure and happiness. It amuses and flabbergasts people who are about my same age to see me skipping rope like Rocky and doing one-armed push-ups. I still abide by the wisdom in the old Greek ideal of a strong mind in a strong body. But perhaps most importantly, it connects me to my more physical, feral ancestors, who appreciated on a visceral level what lithe, strong, quick, and smart animals they were.

And of all the forms of exercise, swimming is the most connected to Nature. When you do yoga or lift weights or sprint, you never feel like you are IN the air. But when you swim, you are unmistakably IN the water. You are immersed in Nature—

both metaphorically and literally.

After the relaxing swim, I pulled myself up into my dinghy and noticed that the children and the cayucos had gone. Because the sun had not yet warmed the solar shower, my fresh water rinse was chilly but invigorating. I rested on the cabin top for a few minutes—iguana-style—using the sun and the breeze as my towel.

When I stepped back into the cockpit, a heart-warming surprise awaited me. The children had left a large, plump mango for me. Aside from its wonderful taste, it is also such a beautiful fruit, with its blend of red, yellow and green imitating half of the rainbow. Soon I was feasting on delicious eggs that I had recently bought from some nearby expats. They call their hens "free range jungle chickens." I accompanied this with juicy mango slices and some fresh squeezed OJ and a spot of rum. Sunday brunch at the Ritz could not be more sublime than this.

Soon my contentment was so profound, that it felt like I could almost physically absorb the mellowness of this day and of this sea gypsy life. I moved up under the shade awning behind the mast, and lazily savored whatever meandered by in the sea and in the sky and in my head. That simple act of mango kindness from the children reminded me of my enduring belief in the goodness and generosity of the human spirit.

* * *

Most of my readers—and the majority of you are distant strangers who I will never meet—know very little about me. That is not an accident. I have deliberately revealed very little about my past. Indeed, the biography on the back cover of this book is only 96 words long. This is not because I have something to hide. Instead, it is because I want my thinking and writing to stand alone on their own merit.

But having just said that, there was a chapter in my life that is very relevant to this particular essay/reverie. Believe it or not, I made my living for many years as a street juggler. For over 25 years I was one of the top street performers in San Francisco. One of the highlights of those decades was when I managed to "juggle my way around the world." I left the Golden Gate with a backpack, a small duffel bag full of tricks and $4,000. After circling the globe, I returned to San Francisco 254 days later with $4,400. I had completely financed the trip by passing my hat in many amazing and exotic locales.

The gift of the humble mango had triggered a flood of memories from that journey. In particular, it reminded me of two of the profound lessons from that vagabond year. The first is that, indeed, we are one human family. And the second is that authentic freedom is precious and rare amongst that human family.

When sitting for my Political Science degree in college, I had some impassioned arguments with my professors about conflict in the world. My belief was that ordinary people everywhere could get along fine with each other. They shared common basic concerns such as: Could they support their families? Were all of their loved ones healthy? Did they have work that was fulfilling and not too exhausting? Was the household joyous most of the time? And did their children's future appear even brighter than their own?

My conviction was that these normal people did not care that much about the color of your skin or the country of your birth or whether you worshipped the correct god—or even any god. These types of animosities were almost always incited by political and religious leaders. There are no historical instances in which a nation suddenly woke up one morning and decided to attack another country. This type of bloodlust insanity has to be carefully and maliciously cultivated by despicable tyrants.

My around the world trip proved the correctness of that conviction that my professors had dismissed so flippantly as "just an idealistic theory." My little juggling act opened doors of friendship and understanding wherever I traveled. And it decisively confirmed my belief in the basic kindness and decency of humanity.

My second revelation on that journey was that the vast majority of people in this world are utterly enslaved by the accident of their birth. Most of the wonderful strangers smiling and laughing in my audiences would never have the opportunity to experience the many joys that had already blessed my trip. They would never view a Van Gogh masterpiece in Amsterdam or ride the Trans-Siberian Railway or stand on the Great Wall of China. In fact, most of them would never travel more than a few hundred miles from where they were born. The tragic unfairness of this wounded me in a very deep place. How did our human societies become so distorted that everyone could not have an equal opportunity to expand their horizons and revel in the magical wonders of our pale blue planet? Why could we not have "humans without borders?"

* * *

Realizing that I had involuntarily veered off into "heavy thinking," I went down to the galley and cut up some ingredients for a ceviche. I squeezed in the lime juice and placed it in the fridge, where it would be ready upon my return. It was time to go visit the neighbors. My camera, binoculars and a bottle of water went into my daypack; and off I went for a row.

I peeked into thick mangroves trying to find a tricolor heron that flew past yesterday. I drifted over the reef waiting to see how long it would take the fish to seek the shade of my little dinghy. And I scouted some tall jungle trees looking for the nest of the golden-tailed weaver birds whose distinctive call greeted me each day.

The hours idled by so seamlessly that it startled me to notice that the horizon was beginning to turn saffron as the sun slid into the west. I began rowing back towards *Aventura*, eagerly anticipating the tasty ceviche. But when I was only about 20 yards from home, I abruptly changed course and headed for the beach on Mango Island. That's because I suddenly realized that it had been far too long since I had climbed up a tree—and shaken out some luscious fruit.

Chained to the Cross

*T*HERE IS NO CALENDAR aboard *Aventura*, and I often lose track of what day it is. Actually, down here—south of many borders—the seasons are so similar to each other that I often lose track of what month it is! But I always know when it is Sunday. That's because a veritable armada of cayucos will stream by my boat on their way to church.

A few weeks ago one passed very close, and as always, I waved with neighborly enthusiasm. Seven or eight of the kids waved back just as vigorously. But there was one young, teen-aged girl who responded differently. Apparently she had never been so close to one of these sailing boats, and she studied it carefully. I watched her gaze drift from bow to stern and then from the waterline to the top of the mast. Then she noticed my boat's name, which is the Spanish word for "adventure."

With the cayuco only 10 feet away, I delighted in seeing her happy smile as visions of travel, freedom and exotic else-where's danced in her head. But swiftly her face changed, and I witnessed something that a man in his middle years never wishes to see in the eyes of someone so young. As she looked directly up at me, I watched as her youthful joy was suffocated by despair. There was surrender in that look—the realization that her dreams for a life that could cross over the borders of her birth might never be achieved.

This experience touched me so deeply that I created this little story, which tries to depict what she is experiencing at this threshold moment in her life. And even if this tale is not accurate in the case of this young woman, it surely is for someone else her age—and probably for many, many others out there who also feel caged by the circumstances of their birth.

* * *

I will name her Dolores, which is the Spanish word for "sadness." She was the second born of 8 children. As is often the case, in an effort to keep up with her older brother, she tended to be tomboyish. If he could row the cayuco across the bay in 20 minutes, she would try to do it in 18 minutes. If he caught 4 fish she would strive for 6. But one thing that they did not compete in was sea turtles. They both loved the big creatures, and would drift for hours amongst them in their little native canoe.

For her 10th birthday, her father took her on a turtle-watching trip at a remote beach. As the female labored most of the night laying her eggs and covering them in the sandy nest, the volunteers quietly explained to Dolores the entire process including how the tiny hatchlings will have to race down the beach to the safety of the sea as predator birds and animals attack them.

It was a momentous night in her young life. Besides being inquisitive about the mother turtle, Dolores asked the volunteers many questions about their lives and their dedication to these animals. She learned that a person had to be at least 18 years old and very carefully trained before they could qualify to be turtle beach monitors. She also discovered that some of them were studying marine biology with a specialty in sea turtles. Dolores felt a bit like her beloved turtles that night. She sensed that she had stuck her head out of her own shell and glimpsed her future.

At school she found a helpful teacher who encouraged her and brought her books and magazine articles about the turtles of the sea. The more she learned, the more she wanted to know. Could it be that one day she could go to university and become a marine biologist and then travel the world studying and helping these gentle animals?

* * *

And now at 13 years old, her family cayuco is passing beside *Aventura*. My sweet little boat is the perfect symbol for all that she seeks in life. But it is not just a fairy tale illusion. It is a real thing—tangible evidence that people can voyage to strange new lands, see unusual creatures and savor exotic adventures. And it lives where the turtles live—in the sea.

As her cayuco heads across the bay to the chapel, the young girl pivots and looks back at the lovely *Aventura* once more. Even from 30 yards away I can sense her longing and her sad resignation. She is headed to church, which is supposed to be a joyous and liberating experience. But Dolores is wise beyond her years, and she understands that it does not emancipate her —it enslaves and crushes her.

Yet, even though she intuitively recognizes this, she cannot possibly imagine how masterfully the church orchestrates it. For over 20 centuries they have perfected their subtle incar-ceration methods so brilliantly that the prisoners barely real-ize that they are captives. Allow me to explain how profoundly and malevolently they dominate so many lives around the world.

Here in Latin America, when a baby is born, it is extremely likely that it will be designated as a Catholic child. A few weeks later a baptismal ceremony further reinforces this status. As the little one finds its way in the world it receives loving guid-ance from its parents. It learns that fire and snakes and lightning are dangerous. And it is also taught that mangoes ripe from the tree and fish fresh from the sea are delicious. A bond of sublime trust is formed between parent and child. So when these adults, who have provided so much helpful knowledge about how the world works, also teach it that religion is a good thing, why would the youngster not believe the parents?

And this is further reinforced by the pageantry of the religious services. Things are different inside the church. It is quieter and solemn and reverent. The kids aren't running around wildly, and the person at the front wears very unusual clothes. He gives some sort of fancy speech that the adults all follow carefully. Afterwards, the grown-ups behave as if something important has happened.

So if the child's parents say that religion is a good thing, and if the ceremony at the church is so extraordinary, then it is natural for the kids to accept their place in the flock. And the term "flock" is appropriate here—for the church controls them as thoroughly as a shepherd dominates his sheep.

The keystone of the church's indoctrination is the concept of hell. The young people are relentlessly warned that if they do certain things they will suffer grotesque agony for all of eternity. Most of the "sins" that will condemn a person to this horrible fate are irrelevant to typical kids. After all, they are not going to murder someone or worship false idols or rob the local bank. But as soon as they reach puberty, they get hammered by a Catholic edict that they barely knew even existed. Thou shalt not use birth control.

After the epiphany that Dolores experienced on the beach with the mother turtle, she realized that her desired path in life was different from most of her peers. Although there was much charm in her Indio village life, her dreams swept towards the far horizon. She wanted to venture beyond the boundaries of her birthplace and embrace the wider world. To achieve this, she would need to succeed in both high school and university.

Just when Dolores was recognizing this, she noticed that many of the girls just a few years older than her were suddenly dropping out of high school and having babies. When she asked them why they didn't wait a little longer until they finished school, they confessed that the pleasure of sex was so extraordinary that they couldn't restrain themselves. And since the almighty church insisted that if they used birth control they would burn in hell for a million years, they had risked unwanted pregnancies because sexual passion can be so overpowering.

Because Dolores had not yet reached puberty, she convinced herself that she could forego sexual desire in order to fulfill her dreams. But when those potent universal yearnings started to pulse through her young body, she too felt herself being swept along and she went to her mother seeking guidance. Why can't a person enjoy the wonders of sex, she asked, without having to risk bringing an unwanted child into the world? Since her mom had never questioned such things herself, her only response was, "...because the church says so, and they know what's best."

But with the exquisite vision of her future blurring and darkening before her eyes, that answer was not good enough for Dolores. So she asked the teacher who had been so helpful to her if there wasn't some other way, some other option? As an instructor in a Catholic school, the sympathetic teacher hesitated, but then decided to answer truthfully. She told her bright young student—so overflowing with curiosity about life and the world—that there was another way. She explained that there are reliable and affordable methods of birth control as close as the nearest drug store. And she added that millions and millions of people around the world use them without fear or guilt, because they have not been told that by doing so they will burn forever in hell.

And then the confused young student said, "But if the church cares about us so much, why would it destroy my dreams for the future—my simple dreams that harm no one and can help the turtles?"

The good teacher paused and looked Dolores in the eyes, "Your question is a just and sensible one, but the answer is very complicated. Anything I say will probably confuse you even more. But in only a few more years you will discover the answer for yourself. And it will be much more powerful and valuable to you because you found it on your own!"

* * *

It was only a few days after that conversation with her beloved teacher that Dolores passed by *Aventura* in the family cayuco headed for church. Had I known the source of the anguish that was so clearly visible in her eyes, I might have shouted out something like this:

"The church does not care about you, Dolores. It seeks only to further its own power and interests. Witness how its birth control rules crush your dreams and force you down a life path that you do not desire. Ignore the church. It is a dictatorship that wants to dominate your heart and your mind and your body. Cast it off like a scorpion on a shoe, and race out into that wide world that beckons to you so powerfully. Listen to the murmurings within you. They are the voices of our race and the echoes of the centuries. They will serve you well."

Never Stop Running, Napalm Girl!

*T*HE SEA WAS MILD and soothing as I sailed alone in the western reaches of the Caribbean. It had been four days since my last human contact. Such exile does not disturb me—it comforts me. The wind was light, and the waves were small and melodious—like the cello phrase in a string quartet.

Although quite relaxed, I was also vigilant, because my position was near the busy shipping lanes between the Panama Canal and the Yucatan Channel. Suddenly, I sensed a nearby hazard. My first scan of the horizon revealed nothing. On my second, more careful sweep, I saw her—a gray smudge of a ship, still half below the undulating cusp of the Earth. I took my binoculars from their rack and focused them. What I saw slammed me backwards—both physically and emotionally. She was one of them—a gray, military transport vessel that was all too familiar to me. I had served aboard one—a U.S. Navy ammunition ship in Vietnam.

* * *

I had not willingly done so. I had been drafted just after receiving my bachelor's degree. My first decision was whether to flee to Canada, as my courageous college roommate had done, or to let them take me. My next choice was between a two-year Army enlistment or the four-year Navy sentence. Wishing to neither kill nor be killed because of anyone's insipid "domino theory," I chose the USN. As someone who survived higher education with my capacity for critical thinking still intact, I already knew that war was horrible and this particular one was senseless and despicable. I was not an ideal recruit. The toughest part of my service was being a closet pacifist aboard a ship full of gung-ho pseudo-warriors. And these were the worst kind—the swaggering, macho types, who had the luxury of never facing any real combat. I kept my secret to myself, just as I kept my self to myself. In fact, I do not have a single friend from that chapter of my life. When I would go ashore and meet actual soldiers, they were not gung-ho at all. They were beaten down and regretful and frightened—and wanted only to be away from there... to be home... to be far from all that madness.

I never talk about this with my friends. And it rarely enters my consciousness. But that dark ship on the horizon, transporting munitions and mutilation to who knows which target this time, just staggered me. To ease my anguish, I tried the comfort of my favorite classical music. It didn't work, and neither did dousing myself with buckets of sea water. Although I resisted, I knew that the only way out of my agony was to burrow deeper into it.

* * *

So I brought out her picture. I keep it protected in an envelope hidden in one of my favorite books. I unfolded it tenderly, and gazed one more time at all the evil, meaningless terror of war captured in a single frozen instant from 40 years ago. I spoke to her once more as I had done many other times down the decades, when I needed solace:

"Hello again, Napalm Girl. Keep on running! There must be some place, somewhere, free from this horror and insanity.

You must find that place. You deserve that place. Never stop running!!!"

She is crying out, "Too hot! Too hot!" as she flees. Grotesque flaming jelly from the sky has burned most of the little dress from her nine-year-old body. The rest she ripped off herself as she kept running and screaming "I'm dying! I'm dying!"

When the heroic photographer got to her, she was whimpering, "Water, water." He emptied his canteen on her. With ferocious determination, through insane traffic, he managed to get her to a hospital in Saigon. They said she was so badly burned that she would never live, and they would not accept her. He flashed his Associated Press photo credentials and said, "Don't let this child die or everyone will hear about it!" They took her in. And they saved her.

That Vietnamese photographer, Nick Ut, deeply understood the ravages of war. His older brother, who was his personal hero, had already died photographing the misery of combat. When Nick answered the call of basic human decency and rescued that terrified little girl, he had no idea that on the film in his camera was one of the most profound and powerful photographs of all time. He was only 19 years old.

Even though the immortal Napalm Girl picture touches me in my core being, it's another photo, the one with her mother sitting beside her in the hospital, that truly haunts me. The woman's quiet dignity as she comforts her innocent frightened child overwhelms me. In her noble image, I can see what an almost unbearable burden but blessing it is to be a Woman, and to be a Mother, in this world of torment. And it sickens me to realize that it is almost always men that cause this needless anguish.

Decades later, I can still imagine their likely conversation as the child asks the mother, "What was that horrible fire that fell from the sky?"

And the mom might reply, "It was some terrible new weapon—like a bomb, but different."

"But why did they drop it on us?" asks the little girl. "We were just children and old people hiding in the temple from the planes. We didn't hurt anybody!"

My guess is that the heroic mother, overwhelmed with grief by the sight of her incinerated child, might have said something like this. "I do not know the answer, my beautiful daughter. But I do know that you survived this horrible thing, and your pain will go away and you will heal. And someday, life will be sweet and sensible again. Now, try to go to sleep, and when you awake, I will be right here beside you."

* * *

The dark gray death ship passed a few miles ahead of me and has now disappeared beyond the horizon. But even though it is no longer visible, its malignancy still torments me. I stare again at little Kim's photo in my hands, and ask myself, "How can I best honor her suffering?" And then I realize that what makes her pain-wracked image so universal and so immortal is that it lays bare the true nature of war. And that the best way to repay my gratitude is to use my power as a writer to further expose this loathsome evil.

* * *

Tragically, as I type these words, the war drums are beating again. The Deceiver-in-Chief has scheduled a national address in which he will knowingly lie about the need for this latest "regrettable but necessary action." Then the commentators will babble on about "sufficient justification" and "reprisals" and "surgical strikes". But they will never discuss what war actually is. And that is because, at its core, it is sick and perverted and senseless.

If someone invades your home and threatens your family, it is your right and your responsibility to protect them, even if it necessitates violence. This type of personal duty is decent, courageous and just. But war is the killing of human beings with whom we have no personal grievance. War is Mass Psychotic Hypnosis. But it is never initiated by ordinary people. One morning at breakfast, a million Norwegians do not spontaneously decide that it would be a good idea to invade Ireland that afternoon.

No, this type of insanity can only be seeded and nurtured by certifiable sociopaths. Unfortunately, we don't call them lunatics and banish them to asylums. Instead, we anoint them as political and religious leaders. These diseased power-addicts use cold-blooded manipulation to convince enormous groups of people that other groups of people are their enemies... and so they must go forth... and annihilate them.

Here is another truth about war that the self-righteous talking heads deliberately avoid: Those who make the wars never have to fight the wars. The Great Deciders will never be in a night ambush, where the fear is so overpowering that their bodily control abandons them and they shit themselves. And the defense contractors, engorged on obscene profits, will never have to kick open a mud hut door after strafing it with automatic weapons fire, and discover a heap of dead children beneath a wounded mother, who is so traumatized that she cannot even scream. And the media tycoons cheerleading for more carnage will never rush to the flag-draped coffin of a dead son or daughter and wrap themselves around it in fury as the military band tries to sound heroic.

And here is yet another profound truth that the acceptable, credentialed pundits never state: War doesn't work! It never makes the world a better place. For thousands of years, humanity has waged hundreds of wars, but they never achieve their supposedly noble ideals. They never "end all wars" or "bring everlasting peace" or "ensure self-determination" or any of the dozen other excuses that are used to incite people to massacre one another. What it does succeed at doing is bringing misery, murder, mutilation and madness to ordinary, decent people.

So listen carefully as the highly-paid military and political analysts parade across your television screens, proclaiming the need for this latest "kinetic action." Observe how these shrewd distorters evade the three paramount characteristics of war that I have just discussed. None of them will address what war really is. Nor will they mention that those who benefit from war do not suffer its horrors. And finally, they will not admit that war never brings good into the world and is actually a plague that sickens the human project.

* * *

Recognizing that war is Mass Psychotic Hypnosis, how do we overcome those who mesmerize us? How do we break free from their spell? Certainly our liberation will not come from those at the top. War rewards them too handsomely.

We must rely on our numbers. We are many, they are few. When the chant from the anti-Vietnam protests, "Hell, no...we won't go!" became a reality and not just a slogan, the war machine sputtered and died. Refusal is our best strategy. We must refuse to serve in their militaries or in their terror cells. We must refuse to resolve disputes through violence. And if they incarcerate us for our resistance, that is a better fate than killing someone who is not an enemy. And when enough of us refuse, their prisons are not large enough to hold us.

I am perfectly mindful that such thinking is idealistic and foolhardy, but perhaps it will inspire others to come forth with better options for ending war. Yet, even if such ideals are useless, we must try—if for no other reason than to honor Kim Phuc, the Napalm Girl. We must sculpt a world where an innocent little girl does not have to race down a road with the flesh peeling off her body, trying to outrun her own death!

The Sea Gypsy Tribe

A FINE SUNSET is beginning to pastel the sky. I am seated on *Aventura*'s cabin top watching a great blue heron standing motionless in the twilight shadows, patiently awaiting its dinner. The melancholy is heavy on me tonight. These pristine, quiet, un-peopled places do that to me.

My sweet, strong sailboat and I have been together for over a quarter of a century. While aimlessly meandering amidst some fond memories of our decades together, I am suddenly jolted by an unpleasant realization: It is all so profoundly different now. When we first sailed together, she was just a seagoing magic carpet, transporting me to faraway lands, plush with exotic creatures and cultures. But now she has also become a survival pod, protecting me from the possibility of societal collapse.

Admittedly, when I first disconnected from life on the land, the world was already extremely dysfunctional. That was part of the enchantment of the sea gypsy life—that I could voluntarily exile myself from much of the violence, injustice, ugliness and shallowness of modern techno-industrial society.

But in only 25 years, global conditions have gone from deeply disturbing to cataclysmic. We certainly knew back then that our human activities were damaging Mother Earth, but we didn't realize that our conduct could actually unravel the critical bio-geo-physical systems that sustain all life on our luxuriant garden planet. Who would have believed that we could actually annihilate our support system?

I might not have believed it back then, but I certainly do now. That's because sailing the wide waters imposes a heightened sense of reality on a person—far more so than shore-side life. Out on the vast ocean, where one has to fend for oneself without any nearby assistance, delusions can kill you. So, my many years at sea have trained me to see things as they are rather than as I wish them to be. And what this sea gypsy beholds just beyond the horizon is grave and frightening.

Fortunately, others far wiser than me also see the troubles ahead, and they are attempting to raise the alarm about the impending catastrophes. But tragically, they are almost completely ignored. This neglect is so significant that I have created a term to describe these well-intentioned messengers who carry such unwelcome news. I call them the Cassandra Choir, because they suffer the same ignoble fate that befell the mythological character Cassandra. She could accurately foretell the future and she used this gift to warn her people about the woes that awaited them. But they either ignored or scorned her.

The truth-tellers of our modern Cassandra Choir are relentlessly marginalized and ridiculed by The Malignant Overlords. These political, corporate, religious and media gatekeepers are so obscenely engorged with wealth and power under the existing system that they will fight ruthlessly to defend the status quo. They desire a population of The Asleep. They fear a population of The Awake.

So they label those in the Choir "screwball doomers" and claim that the risks that they are exposing are greatly exaggerated, and they do their utmost to ensure that the message of the Cassandra Choir is suppressed, because, when looked at objectively, it is supremely convincing. (At the end of this essay I will provide a list of many of these insightful and courageous thinkers. A few weeks spent reading them will probably convince you that our current path will most likely lead to a devastating societal collapse.)

* * *

The phrase that I use to describe the possible catastrophes confronting us is the Big Bad E's, which stand for Energy, Economy and Ecology. One of these alone could destabilize the world so profoundly that the life that we currently take for granted would be shattered. But because they are so intertwined, an emergency in one will probably impact the others, thus compounding and accelerating the problem.

Let's look at Energy first. Any clear thinker can discern that Petroleum has virtually enslaved us. Its black hand is smeared across every aspect of our daily routines. Without abundant, affordable liquid fuels, the food trucks stop delivering to the grocery stores, the tractors aren't plowing the fields, the airplanes don't fly, and the container ships can't transport low-priced consumer goods from East to West. And, even more disastrously, a large portion of the power grid goes down. Without electricity, the air conditioners don't cool and all of the electronic gadgetry that mesmerizes the citizenry into a docile stupor suddenly disappears. The swiftness with which the fabric of civil society can be shredded will be astonishing.

As for Economics, because of the interconnected nature of our globalized world, a crisis in one area will impact billions on the other side of the planet. Should China decide to renounce the U.S. dollar as the world reserve currency and install its own gold-backed yuan, this will have profound repercussions in every nation and in every market, whether it is stocks, bonds or commodities.

The Ecological future looks even more terrifying each passing month: melting ice caps, further destruction of the Amazonian rainforest, bubbling tundra, and a relatively new environmental horror—climate change denial—add up to a grim path forward... and most likely downward.

These are just a few "scribbled on a napkin" examples of possible disasters headed our way that easily came to mind because of my years of researching the likelihood of Collapse. Anyone who thoroughly investigates the existing data is likely to reach a similar conclusion—that we are probably doomed. Almost the entire Cassandra Choir agrees in this regard. A huge die-off of billions of people and a reset to an almost unrecognizable, low-tech style of living seems to be the consensus.

And the most radical sector of the Choir is so pessimistic that they have coined the acronym NTHE, which stands for "Near Term Human Extinction." They believe that Homo sapiens will either go completely extinct, or only a few pockets of a remnant population will survive. I ardently hope that this is not the case, and my research up to this point has not totally convinced me that this is inevitable. But there is a wise old sailors' adage that goes like this: "Hope for the best, but prepare for the worst!"

It is in this profoundly empowering spirit that I have written the rest of this essay. Up to this point it has just been an introduction, a setting of the scene. The rest of this meditation is my core message and my heartfelt truth. I hope it proves to be a helpful addition to the growing conversation on how we can most wisely confront the agony that lies ahead.

* * *

Many members of the Cassandra Choir paint a sobering and convincing portrait of the horrors that are headed our way. The unsettling images in their books and blogs are so disturbing that they often feel obligated to conclude their message on a more cheerful and optimistic note. So they usually extol the value of "resilient communities" that can protect their members from the ravages that most people will experience.

I greatly admire the basic concepts behind this Transition Town/permaculture/low-tech model. But sadly, I believe that this response to an imploding world is as doomed as the "stay in the city and see what happens" approach. The reason for my concern can be stated in one word—marauders! As a friend of mine tragically describes it, "The Amish are toast." When people are cornered into choosing between starving and marauding, it is fairly easy to predict their decision. This is a recurring blind spot in the otherwise brilliant and well-grounded thinking of the Cassandra Choir. How can they not foresee that their vegetable gardens and root cellars and chicken coops will be stormed and ravaged by heavily-armed, hungry people?

But the solution that I am proposing to any worst-case Collapse scenario deals with the problem of marauders effortlessly—you simply sail away from the violence and mayhem that is overwhelming both the cities and the countryside. I call my alternative approach The Sea Gypsy Tribe.

Name any apocalyptic scenario, and I will argue that being at sea in a sailing vessel is the best way to deal with it. Pandemic? The contagion danger comes from large groups of humans jammed closely together. Grid Down? Sailboats can be made into self-contained survival pods with wind and solar power systems, water-makers and long-distance radios. Thermonuclear? There is not a single ICBM on the planet aimed towards the middle of the ocean. And the fallout danger is more easily handled in a boat with ¾ of its surface area underwater. Famine? It is easy to have a year's worth of provisions stashed onboard, and the sea provides fish, shellfish and seaweed. Submerged Coastal Cities? Not an issue in a floating survival module.

But more than just being a survival concept, I also envision the Sea Gypsy Tribe as a "seeding" option. Here is my basic premise:

> **I believe that if there is
> a near-extinction catastrophe,
> a Sea Gypsy Tribe has the best chance
> of both surviving and replenishing
> the human population in the wisest manner.**

Those last four words are exceedingly important—"in the wisest manner." There is already a fairly large group of people who have been paying attention to the global unraveling and have responded by preparing for the worst. These folks are usually referred to as "preppers." I applaud their foresight and dedication, but I have grave doubts about their ability to reboot the post-Collapse emergent world "in the wisest manner."

That's because most of the preppers are very religious and patriotic. And there is overwhelming evidence that more blood has been shed in human history in the name of god and country than for any other cause. And besides that, the hierarchal nature of religions and nations invariably attracts the most ambitious, ruthless sociopaths who ascend to the highest positions of power. They would soon be repeating the same mistakes that plague us today.

* * *

What I propose is a far bolder vision of a post-Collapse future. I call it Humanity 3.0. Our hunter/gatherer ancestors were Humanity 1.0, and our civilized forebears comprised Humanity 2.0. For about 2 million years the Paleolithic tribes lived peaceably with each other and in balance with Nature. They perceived the world as a web and themselves as but one strand amongst millions of others. They lived a life of harmony rather than hegemony.

But then about 10,000 years ago, at the onset of what I term "conquest agriculture," humanity drastically changed its philosophy. These Neolithic villagers started viewing all of Life as a pyramid with Homo sapiens at the pinnacle. And they perceived this position as a justification for ruling over all of the other life forms on the planet. This marked the beginning of what we term Civilization. It also marked the arrival of States and Churches and Rulers and Priests. As this worldview expanded and accelerated it unleashed dire consequences for all life-forms, and now it even jeopardizes our future existence as a species. I discuss the disastrous, unintended consequences of Civilization in much greater detail in my essay entitled "The Vast Picture," which was the first essay I wrote in this series.

I believe that the Sea Gypsy Tribe can function like the monks of the Dark Ages, who preserved the best of the Greek and Roman cultures, which then led to the Enlightenment and to the Renaissance. Our mission would be to conserve the best of Humanity 2.0, and also to sound the alarm about its worst elements. I have a catchphrase to describe this—"Mozart without the mushroom cloud."

* * *

Perhaps the best aspect of my Sea Gypsy Tribal concept is that it is achievable. It does not require a global paradigm shift. It just needs about 1,000 kindred spirits. I use that arbitrary number because many anthropologists believe that after the last great human extinction event—the Toba volcanic eruption, approximately 77,000 years ago—there were only about 1,000 survivors, and yet they successfully managed to repopulate the planet.

Right now there are already tens of thousands of people scattered around our wet, lush planet living a full-time sailing life. The vast majority of them do not possess what I would consider essential Sea Gypsy Tribe values, but there is probably a tiny minority that is ripe and anxious for my message. We just need to find each other, discover our common philosophical beliefs, and exchange contact info. Then, if things start deteriorating, the various seagoing tribes can come together in their particular neighborhood of Mother Ocean. A simple means of identification is the Earth Flag. I have been flying mine for decades. It symbolizes my desire for a world without borders. Anyone displaying the Earth Flag is probably an excellent candidate for the Sea Gypsy Tribe.

* * *

So, what sort of paradigm shift in values would I wish to see in this new, water-borne community? I'll gladly provide some examples, but I emphasize that I am vehemently against "imposing" a philosophy on anyone. My goal is to inspire. I believe in "suggestions" and I despise "commandments!" If I was a Sea Gypsy Tribal Elder, here are some of the things that I would recommend to my clan. They could then choose whether or not to embrace them.

• **Humanity's Place In The Scheme Of Things**. We have tried to elevate ourselves above the other creatures on our planet by claiming that we are human "beings." But we are actually just human *animals*. We have further deceived ourselves by claiming that the geometry of life is a pyramid, and we humans are at the apex. So this entitles us to dominate and control everything else—including the creatures, the land, the water and the air. We must return to the geometry that our Humanity 1.0 hunter/gatherer ancestors so clearly understood—that life is a web and damaging one strand damages the whole.
• **The Limits Of Growth**. Only a buffoon believes that there can be infinite growth, which requires infinite resource ex-

traction, on a finite planet. But beyond the absurdity of the equation, there is also the atrocity of its perspective. The few dozen indigenous tribes still surviving on our blighted, techno-industrial planet view the rivers, forests and mountains as their living neighbors. They don't see them as commodities—as hydroelectric power, as board-feet or as open-pit mines. Gaia should be enjoyed, cherished and protected—not strip-mined!

• **A World Of Too Much Technology Cannot Be Repaired With More Technology.** The Luddites in England and the last Samurai in Japan were correct—the seductive benefits of techno-industrial Civilization would be short-lived. But the horrors that they spawned would be forever. The 443 nuclear reactors in the USA are a testament to this. It takes about 10 years to decommission each one. What will happen if the power grid goes down swiftly and all those cooling ponds dry up? We should abandon our addiction to "the latest gadget" and embrace low or appropriate technology. A basic, any-ocean sailboat is a great example of this. It is a bridge across to the Old Ways. Or as I like to say, "The path to the Future leads to the Past!"

• **Immersion In Nature Is A Necessity And Not A Luxury.** None of the 80-90 indigenous tribes still living in their native habitats suffer from mental illness, require psychiatrists, or need psychotropic drugs. Our Paleolithic operating system is designed for living in "the Wild" and not in human-built environments. I get to spend long periods alone with the creatures of the sea and the sky. To me this is not a vacation, it is a vital psychic centering. We must come home to the wild.

• **Hierarchal Societies Become Horrible Societies.** Tribal societies are small bands where everyone knows each other and they work together for the good of the clan. There are no rulers and ruled, no rich and poor, no inequality between the sexes, and no chiefs living in splendor while the rest live in squalor. But hierarchal societies suffer from all of those injustices. And despite the false propaganda, those who rise to power in hierarchies are not usually the "best and the brightest." More often they are the most ambitious, ruthless and despicable, thus leading to "dominator" cultures that spew death and destruction across the planet. Hierarchies should be as unwelcome as the bubonic plague.

• **Capitalism Must Capsize.** It should be obvious that any system that places profit ahead of both people and the planet will end up being a disaster for both. Any economic model that worships greed, cannot possibly serve the common interest or the greater good. The tribal model has provided fulfilling lives without jeopardizing the environment for two million years. Shouldn't we dismantle a system which only enriches a tiny elite, and in just a few centuries is destroying the ecosystem which we depend on for our very survival?

• **Churches And States Must Stay Buried In The Ashes.** The most obscene atrocities in human history have usually been committed in the name of the love of god or the love of country. There is nothing wrong with striving for spiritual joy, but organized religions that demonize other groups and command their annihilation should never re-emerge from the Collapse. As for States, humanity existed contentedly for two million years without them. And in only 10,000 years since their arrival we have massacred hundreds of millions of people, and now are on the verge of decimating our planetary support system. Churches and States should be buried for eternity in the world's most polluted toxic waste sites.

If I was a Tribal Elder at a Council of Deciding, these are the far-reaching changes that I would recommend to my people. They may seem radical, but I perceive them as "radically sensible." Also, it should be remembered that these proposals are designed for a future scenario where there has been a cataclysmic societal collapse and the survivors are attempting to rebuild a civilization far more enlightened than our current version.

* * *

But let's hope that we are never in that position. A huge majority of my personal friends regard my views on the possibility of impending collapse as semi-lunatic. They agree that the world is enormously screwed up, but they believe that humanity will continue to muddle along with things steadily deteriorating, and then some miracle will come along and save us. I would be delighted if they are right and I am wrong. But if they *are* correct, I still encourage people to consider adopting the Sea Gypsy Tribal Path as perhaps the healthiest way of living on a very diseased planet. These are some of its many rewards that I know so well from my decades of Sea Gypsy living:

• You are a World Citizen and thus in no way supporting the imperialistic perversions of any government.
• You live in the Yellow Light rather than the Blue Light. Your illumination comes from Mother Sun and not from electronic addiction devices.
• You can escape the steady defilement of daily life as world governments keep morphing into police-surveillance states.
• You can reconnect with and embrace anew your wild, animal self.
• You can live slowly and simply—immersed in nature—and exiled from the meaningless frenzy of the so-called real world.
• You can discover anew a sense of connectedness as you mesh with your new tribe of kindred spirits.

* * *

I hope that my words and my vision will inspire some of you out there to consider the Sea Gypsy Tribe as a viable alternative to a possible disastrous future. My desire with this article was to introduce an entirely new and potentially successful approach to worst-case-scenario survival strategy. But to state it more poetically, my heart of hearts hope is... that this little essay will launch a fleet of a thousand Thoreaus.

Author's Note: As promised here are some members of the Cassandra Choir. The topics that they emphasize in their thinking and writing include: Collapse, Peak Everything, Downside of Civilization, Economic Lunacy, Eco-Disaster and How the World Really Works. This is by no means an all-inclusive list, but it will give anyone with a sincere interest in re-evaluating the Future, a lot of wise resource material.

Dmitry Orlov, James Howard Kunstler, Richard Heinberg, Chellis Glendinning, Guy McPherson, Carolyn Baker, Derrick Jensen, Daniel Quinn, Morris Berman, John Zerzan, Jerry Mander, Jared Diamond, Howard Zinn, Albert Bates, Naomi Klein, Jan Lundberg, Paul Craig Roberts, Chris Hedges, Michael Ruppert, George Mobus, Dave Pollard, David Korten, Bill McKibben, William Catton, Thomas Berry, Tyler Durden, Matt Simmons, Stacy Herbert, Max Keiser, Gail Tveberg, Gerald Celente, Joseph Tainter, Ronald Wright, William Banzai and many more fine and courageous thinkers...

Enslaved by Our Stuff

*W*E WERE STILL... and we were solitary. The wind had been mute for two days. Our only companions were our brethren in the sea and the sky. No other human presence disturbed this deep blue mirror, stretching to the horizon. *Aventura* and I were becalmed but content.

I rigged a shade awning and went below for a chilled drink. My tiny refrigerator is powered by a solar panel. A cold young coconut was awaiting me. I opened it with my machete, inserted a straw and savored it beneath the awning. My back rested against the mast and my thoughts drifted as aimlessly and contentedly as my boat. Gradually, the word "contentment" inspired a meditation on what I consider one of the great curses of the modern world ... Stuff.

We have been led to believe that acquiring more stuff brings us greater freedom and happiness. I heartily disagree, and to support my position I will call three wise men as witnesses. Here is Thoreau's opinion on the subject: "A man is rich in direct proportion to the number of things that he can live without." Mark Twain had an apt quote on the issue as well: "We have turned a thousand useless luxuries into necessities." And Bertrand Russell was even more emphatic with this quotation:

"It is our preoccupation with possessions, more than anything else, that prevents us from living freely and nobly."

In other words, we are enslaved by our stuff! And it is more insidious and malignant than traditional slavery, because we are not forced to submit to this enslavement, we voluntarily do so. Materialism has become the true worldwide religion. If most people were told that for the rest of their lives they could only go to either the church or the mall, which would they select? They would choose the Temple of Shopping.

What makes this situation even more tragic is that our worship of stuff is not just some innocent, unavoidable human trait. Almost any anthropologist who has spent time amongst the 85 or so indigenous tribes who still survive far from the tentacles of industrial-techno civilization will verify that there is an amazing lack of private property amongst these (misnamed) primitives. They possess very little stuff, and much of what they do have is communally shared. So, this greed for things, which consumes modern humanity, is not intrinsic to our nature. It is manipulated into us.

And the exploiters who condemn us to the treadmill of "more, more and still more" do not do this benevolently. Their motive is to further enrich themselves and to increase their control over us. Does the concept of "planned obsolescence" profit the makers of the products, or does it benefit the consumers of these items? After you have answered that obvious question, step back a bit further and ponder how we have allowed ourselves to be reduced to the status of "consumers."

Our culture programs us so thoroughly and yet so subtly that we do not even perceive our captivity. Just as the fish is unaware of the water that it is immersed in, humanity is unmindful of the severity of its enslavement. Certainly the desperately poor in the world realize that they are captives to the daily struggle for survival, but the more well-to-do have also lost much of their freedom. Consider this downward human trajectory:

Our hunter/gatherer ancestors survived independently for over a hundred thousand years using their amazing physical and mental powers in a fairly hostile world. When they encountered a mirror-like pond, they could look at their reflection and see a strong, lithe, smart, human animal that could fend for itself and protect its tribe.

But with the advent of agriculture came the ascension of rulers and priests. These ruthless manipulators swiftly recognized that in order to exploit the human animal, they would need to domesticate it. A person that could feed, clothe, shelter and protect herself or himself would not consent to subjugation. So the rulers imposed dependency through division of labor. The hide tanner relied on the barley grower who needed the well-digger who depended on the tool-maker. Life became compartmentalized and the subtle slavery began.

Shortly after that came a further diminishing of the wondrous, free, and empowered human animal. This arrived with the imposition of political boundaries. People were now designated as Assyrians or Egyptians or Babylonians. Next, came the religious divisions which further reduced human autonomy. So the wild, independent, almost feral human animal had now been domesticated so thoroughly that they had morphed into a citizen and a churchgoer. What a sad and pathetic degradation.

And as the human caravan continues down the centuries, rulers and priests still dominate us. They constantly rein in our independence as they transform us into serfs or slaves or soldiers or salesmen. And now, without even realizing it, we are suffocating beneath the ultimate indignation. We have been degraded so profoundly that we don't even cringe when we are called consumers. Step out of the cultural programming bubble and contemplate that. On the one luxuriant planet amongst millions of dead ones, we are the most highly-evolved species, and yet we spend our brief time here... *shopping*. This is insanely tragic and repellent. It is also why the few dozen hunter/gatherer tribes still in existence feel sorry for us. And why they do not wish to adopt our "civilized" ways.

* * *

The mandate to "buy, buy and buy some more" is so all-pervasive in our society that it is difficult to even notice it, much less escape it. But emancipation *is* possible. Through the help of Thoreau, Twain and Russell, I managed to liberate myself. Perhaps, as homage to these wise ones, I can help a few of you to unshackle yourselves. Settle in for a few minutes and let me acquaint you with some of the Evils of Materialism that the consumer culture cheerleaders never mention:

• **We Are Not Our Stuff.** People who wish to get rich by selling us things that we do not need try to convince us that unless we purchase the hot new item we will be conspicuously inferior to our peers. They are trying to manipulate us into the belief that a person's character corresponds to the size of their stuff-pile. Things become status symbols. Because my car is pricier than yours, then I am a better person. But only an advertising-addled fool believes that, for the most successful accumulators of stuff are usually the most ambitious, immoral and ruthless members of society. Almost everyone knows in their heart of hearts that the qualities that are the true measure of a person's worth have nothing to do with stuff. Character traits like wisdom, compassion, serenity, humor and subtlety of mind will always surpass garish mansions and shiny cars.

• **Stuff-Less Happiness.** I have fewer things than almost anybody I know, and yet on a day-to-day basis, I am happier than almost anybody I know. In fact when people visit my boat for the first time there is often an awkward silence as their eyes glance around the cabin. Then they will sheepishly ask, "Ray, where's all your stuff?" My honest answer is that indeed,

I am poor in stuff, but I am rich in time, friendship, health, adventure, freedom, relaxation, travel, etc. This perspective is reinforced as I watch the nearby Indio kids play joyously with just a stick and a coconut, while the ex-pat kids are cursing at their "Eternal Fun" app that isn't working.

• **Consumers Versus Thinkers.** Those who have gained control of any society do not want the vast majority of the people to engage in critical thinking. If the population did so, they would no longer tolerate the obscene wealth disparity or the ever-growing police/surveillance grid or a reverse Robin Hood economy that robs the poor to give to the Wall Street rich. So the citizenry must be distracted and placated. Stuff is the opiate that the Elites use to defuse any rebellious tendencies. Give them gigantic plasma TVs and iEverythings and the latest violent video game and they can control them like two-legged sheep.

• **Stuff Strangles Integrity.** When I was in Vietnam I often tried to unravel the mystery of how anyone could invent napalm and still live with himself. It took me decades to realize that even that horrendous depravity was connected to our worship of stuff. The thinking runs like this: Since everyone else has nice houses and new cars and the latest HDTVs, then I need those things too, in order to maintain my self-respect. Therefore, if the job pays enough, I will just ignore the consequences of what I am inventing. So even though this high-tech weapon causes grotesque tomato-sized tumors on innocent children, I will rationalize that away with the delusion that I am spreading democracy. But if stuff wasn't so godlike, more people would refuse to accept despicable jobs just because they pay well.

• **Consumerism Is Consuming The Planet.** By worshipping stuff and embracing an extravagant, constant-growth lifestyle we are poisoning the air, fouling the rivers, sweeping away the topsoil, decimating the ocean fisheries and generally wreaking havoc on our biosphere. Those 85 indigenous tribes are not doing this. It is our shop-till-you-drop mindset that is fueling this human engine of destruction.

* * *

I lost track of time as I pondered these things, and was momentarily startled when my thoughts returned from the real world to this, my preferred world. *Aventura* and I were still becalmed, but as she knows even better than me, the sea is never truly still. The undulating movement is so minuscule and yet so monumental that it seems like the pulse of the planet. It comforts me deeply, because it feels like Gaia is breathing.

In Praise of Pantheism

*I*T HAS BEEN 23 years since a mystical experience jolted my consciousness. But the memory of that event remains so vivid that it could have been only 23 seconds ago. *Aventura* and I were westbound in the immense Pacific. There was no land within a thousand miles in any direction.

Several dolphins had surrounded us, but they were behaving in a strange manner. Instead of frolicking in the bow wave as they normally do, they were repeatedly circling from bow to stern. I tried to decipher this, and guessed that they were pointing out the majestic full moon looming directly ahead.

Or perhaps they were agitated by the powerful rain squall that had just ended.

Suddenly, a particularly large dolphin approached to within a few feet, pivoted its body, and actually looked me in the eye. Mesmerized, I followed its path as it circled back behind the boat. And there, emblazoned across the sky in shimmering magnificence, was a moon bow! Bands of luminous silver, opaque white and misty lavender arched across the eastern horizon.

I shouted my thanks to the dolphins for alerting me to this phenomenon that very few people ever witness. And then a staggering awareness overwhelmed me. I realized that of the billions of humans on Planet Earth, because of my mid-ocean isolation, I was probably the only one witnessing this exquisite spectacle.

* * *

Soon the moon bow dissipated and the clouds dispersed. The universe dispatched its million twinkling messengers to remind me of its incomprehensible vastness. Lying on my back, on the deck of my tiny boat, in this gigantic ocean, on a small planet, in this immeasurable cosmos, I received my baptism as a pantheist. It was at that moment that I excommunicated myself from human-created gods and embraced the sanctity of Nature and the glory of the Universe. This majesty —this mystery—this miracle—seemed truly worthy of human reverence.

And as I now peer at our world, 23 years later, the value of pantheism is even more evident, since humans continue to slaughter each other in the name of their multitude of "one true gods." Whether it is Muslims against Christians or Shiites versus Sunnis or Tamils battling Hindus, our planet is awash in unnecessary bloodshed.

And yet it is all so easily avoidable. Name one war ever fought in the name of pantheism!!! But if I asked you to list some of the evils directly linked to human-spawned gods, the catalog would be long and horrible. It would include:

- Religious wars and crusades
- Witch hunts
- Persecutions of "infidels"
- Torture
- Human sacrifice
- Fostering the terrifying myth of Hell
- Burnings-at-the-stake
- Rejection of scientific discoveries

- Suicide bombers
- Demonization of our natural sexuality
- Claiming that innocent babies are born guilty of the Original Sin.
- Forcing unwanted children on poor, overburdened parents by threatening eternal hellfire
- Justification for slavery
- Reducing females to a subservient status to males

What a dreadful cavalcade of atrocities has been visited upon the world and its creatures in the name of organized religions! The defenders of these faiths often justify these horrors by claiming that churches are necessary because they provide a moral foundation for the world. The absurdity of such a claim would be comical if it wasn't so tragic.

Look again at that litany of terrors and ask yourself this: "Could any of them be committed in the name of the love of Nature or in the name of basic human decency?" Of course not, but they *all* have been committed in the name of somebody's favorite god. And this continues right up to this very moment. In fact, as I type this sentence, somewhere in the world an innocent child is probably being killed or mutilated because of religious fanaticism.

* * *

Let us consider the roots of religion. Our early ancestors were surrounded by inexplicable, terrifying forces such as thunder, lightning, floods, volcanoes, earthquakes and hurricanes. Because of their limited knowledge, they suspected that these horrors were caused by invisible gods. And in order to obtain the mercy of these gods, they paid homage to them in various ways. So the original "religious impulse" was a survival strategy.

But with the arrival of what I call Conquest Agriculture about 10,000 years ago, religion changed from a survival strategy to an "exploitation strategy." Food surpluses eliminated the hunter/gatherer lifestyle, and led to social hierarchies, divisions of labor and the disastrous emergence of rulers and priests. These early religious tyrants realized that they could gain enormous power and wealth if they claimed to be intermediaries between the gods and the frightened people.

But when reason and science were able to prove that thunder, lightning, floods, etc. were not unleashed by unknowable behind-the-scenes gods but through very knowable natural laws, the priests should have disappeared. After all, there was no longer a need for human emissaries to non-existent gods. But the bishops and mullahs and rabbis were not willing to surrender their wealth and power. So, in order to keep the "con" going, they played the "enemy" card. As long as the people could be convinced that other religions were a threat, then the need for priests could continue. It is a vile charade forced upon us by power-junkie psychopaths.

* * *

Allow me to demonstrate how pantheism can break the spell of these conjurers. But first I will clearly define what pantheism is for me. It is not the "god is everywhere" version. On the contrary, it is the "god is nowhere, but Nature is everywhere" variety. It permits me to exhibit reverence towards something that is indisputably authentic and evident as opposed to worshipping a being whose existence cannot even be proven. Now let me describe its many positive and powerful aspects.

There is no "enemy" in pantheism. People don't go to war over who has the most beautiful waterfalls. There is no need for all of the trappings of institutional religion. Who needs cathedrals and mosques on a planet lush with redwood forests and pristine shorelines? All of the money spent on such prideful glorification could be allocated to far more important needs such as universal clean drinking water or birth control that does not diminish pleasure.

Pantheists do not dictate how people should conduct their lives. There are no commandments from invisible sky bosses. Caring deeply about the planet and all of its creatures is a far wiser ethical foundation than rules supposedly imposed by a dictator in the clouds who is paranoid that his human pawns might worship false idols.

Pantheists enjoy fuller and richer daily lives because they don't view this existence as a dress rehearsal for some heavenly paradise. This is it, so we embrace it with vibrant enthusiasm. We are also not obsessed with the "How did this all happen?" issue. The wonders of the Cosmos are no less magical and amazing just because we cannot fully comprehend them. They are still holy, and worthy of our reverence.

Pantheism also provides a fulfilling alternative for the many borderline atheists out there who recognize the absurdity and evil in organized religion but are troubled by the lack of spirituality in atheism. Although Richard Dawkins is a pre-eminent atheist, when I hear him speak about the wonders to be found through the microscope and the telescope, he sounds to me like a pantheist poster boy.

* * *

Finally, let me revisit the title of this essay—In Praise of Pantheism. I have tried to convince you that pantheism is the ideal spiritual practice for our present, troubled era. It eliminates all of the horrors of institutional religions that I listed earlier, and yet it fulfills our need for something outside of ourselves that is extraordinary and worthy of adoration. At a time when human activities are destroying our very life support system, how can we not turn to a sacred path that reveres our great mother, the Earth, and worships her great mother, the Universe?

Encouragement for
a Young Nonconformist

*T*HE SKY WAS as dark and nasty as the soul of a Dostoyevsky villain. Huge, powerful clouds that looked like charcoal dipped in molten lead were blasting down the mountainside towards *Aventura*. I let out more anchor chain and checked the deck for any loose items. Then I went below to await the tempest. It did not disappoint! Fierce wind ushered in rain as strong as a tropical waterfall. After 20 minutes the worst of it passed and the sky lightened to a sort of pewter gray. The rain decreased from torrential to steady.

This was the perfect accompaniment for my present task. I had just responded to a heartfelt email from an unknown teenager who found solace in my writing. He was struggling with the awareness that he was different from most of his classmates, and that he did not fit in. High school can be a very cruel environment for someone who does not conform. I sent him an encouraging email, but then realized that there are so many others in their formative years who are battling the same demons. And so I decided to write an essay dealing with their difficulties in the hopes of bolstering both their spirits and their resolve.

* * *

This is familiar psychological territory for me. A focal point of my own youth had been my recognition that I was unusual. It wasn't so severe that I felt like an outcast; nor was it so ennobled that I viewed myself as a crusading rebel. Instead, I just knew—vaguely but with certainty—that I was different.

I tended to look at things more deeply—to analyze words and actions carefully in an attempt to see what was really going on. And my emotional sensitivity gave me a low tolerance for strife. Family arguments that might easily be laughed off by other temperaments weighed very heavily on me.

On a less personal level, when I looked around the world I saw a planet of astonishing beauty and riches; and yet a human project that was plagued by poverty, injustice and senseless bloodshed. It puzzled and troubled me that a species with so much intelligence and ingenuity could not solve these problems.

The great blessing of those difficult years was my wonderful mother. Even though she only had a minimal education, she seemed to possess maximum wisdom. She never belittled me for my nonconformist way of looking at life. In fact, she vigorously encouraged me to follow my own path—as long as it harmed no one. My mom was an extraordinary nurturer, and she remains a lifelong inspiration.

The reason for this little autobiographical profile is to assure you that as I address this topic it is not just from a theoretical position. I have been there... and I know your agony! So let me share with you the meandering path that I followed which allowed me to cherish my nonconformity rather than regret it.

* * *

Of the various definitions for "philosopher," my favorite has always been "a lover of wisdom." Early in my search for a deeper understanding of the human condition, I discovered three powerful quotations that guided my explorations, helped me navigate through many of life's tribulations, and brought me soothing comfort in dark times. Perhaps they can do the same for you.

The first quote is from Socrates. "The unexamined life is not worth living!" These seven words are so timeless and so illuminating that they have been passed along from generation to generation for over 2,000 years. For the non-conformist these are celebratory words. They empower you to resist just getting swept along by the tides of modern living. They implore you to scrutinize and evaluate those currents.

Most of your peers are addicted to their smartphones or to the Mall or to the latest Miley/Justin/Selena scandal. They probably mock you for perceiving the shallowness of such pursuits and for not joining in. But take comfort in this: almost all human betterment has been empowered by people who were out of step with the herd. Those in the mainstream do not advance the river of human flourishing—they impede it. History is shaped by those on the fringes who disturb the waters with their uncomfortable and inconvenient insights.

Rage on!

The second indispensable quotation that has sculpted my life comes from one of my great heroes, Henry David Thoreau. "A man is rich in direct proportion to the number of things that he can live without." Not only do our possessions end up possessing us, they also suffocate us. If you embrace a life of voluntary simplicity you will not have to spend so much time in the pursuit of money. Instead, you can dedicate yourself to the quest for knowledge.

Too much stuff also robs us of our powers of perception. To truly examine the world, a certain slowness and tranquility is required. Look around you at your peers. Do they seem relaxed and introspective or do they appear frenzied and confused? I recommend that you minimize your desire for possessions which mostly nurture the ego, and maximize your love of philosophy which nourishes the soul.

Simplify on!

The third quote that seared itself into my worldview comes from the great populist mystical poet, Walt Whitman: "Question much—obey little!" Not only are these extremely wise words, they have also proven to be exceedingly prophetic. Almost all of the over-arching elements of the so-called "civilized" world have been grossly corrupted. Government no longer serves the people—it serves the rich. Education doesn't encourage critical thinking—it encourages "hive mind." Capitalism does not "raise all boats"—it drowns the poor people living on the shore. The media does not report the truth—it distorts the truth in order to serve the ruling elites.

It is the nonconformists who have the courage to question the status quo and challenge the dominant paradigm. And with the increasing cleverness and ruthlessness of the Powers That Rule—a far more accurate term than the Powers That Be —in manipulating public perception, the need for alert and brave people of conscience is greater than ever.

Question on!

* * *

Those three wise adages from Socrates, Thoreau and Whitman were immensely valuable in helping me adhere to my own personal path of nonconformity—my own road less traveled. I suspect that they will be equally helpful to you as well. But because the writing of this piece has forced me to visit the misery of my own teenage years, and because I wish for you to experience as little of that as possible, I am now going to share with you some of the contemporary writers who have had a transformative impact on me. None of these sources were available to me when I was your age; and so it is gratifying to be able to acquaint you with their work. There are many more that I could include, but this list will be an excellent primer to get you started. Enjoy!

• **The Real America:** Howard Zinn, Chalmers Johnson, William Blum, Morris Berman, Chris Hedges and Paul Craig Roberts
• **The Ills Of Civilization:** Daniel Quinn, Chellis Glendinning, Derrick Jensen and John Zerzan
• **The Problems With Capitalism:** Michael Parenti, David Korten, John Perkins and Jerry Mander
• **Deep Politics:** Charles Hugh Smith and Peter Dale Scott
• **The Possibility Of Collapse:** Dmitry Orlov, Carolyn Baker, Guy McPherson, James Howard Kunstler, Chris Martenson and Richard Heinberg

* * *

When I had completed the longhand version of this essay, I put down my clipboard and headed topside to see if the sky had cleared. To my astonishment I discovered three little birds skittering happily around my self-steering vane. Had they been up there cavorting for the entire time that I had been writing? I smiled at the image of these three tiny, joy-filled birds playing the role of miniature muses for this often inept philosopher.

The Nobel Peace Prize Deception

*E*VERY OCTOBER I foolishly get my hopes up as the announcement of the Nobel Peace Prize approaches. My dream is that the committee will finally proclaim that the greatest obstacle to world peace is American Imperialism. And then they will elaborate on this by insisting that only when the U.S. Empire has vanished can global harmony and justice prevail. Therefore, they award the prize to some courageous writer or film-maker or activist who has been battling this death-spewing Leviathan.

But once more they have refused to notice the 800-pound War Lord in the middle of the room. They have again chosen the path *most* taken—the spineless one—and bestowed the award on some noble but uncontroversial candidates. By misdirecting our attention away from the indisputably evil scourge that is U.S. foreign policy, they have once again blockaded the road to actual Peace on Earth.

But perhaps I should question why I even expect those at the Nobel to be noble. After all, they somehow forget to bestow the prize on the greatest peacemaker and liberator of the 20th Century—Mahatma Gandhi. And then they intensified the shame of such an oversight by bestowing the award to one of the most genocidal monsters of the same century—Henry

Kissinger. He received the prize even though he masterminded the secret and massive bombing assault on the innocent peasants of Laos and Cambodia. He was also instrumental in enabling the murderous regimes in East Timor and Chile. In all of these atrocities, he denied his involvement until the evidence finally drowned his lies in truth.

Then they award the 2009 prize to newly-elected Barack Obama, who had done exactly *zero* to move the world toward peace. Certainly, he had excelled at delivering altruistic platitudes fed to him via his teleprompter. But his actions desecrate his words. Here are some bullet points that come to mind without even having to do any deep research:

• Obama vowed during his campaign to close down Guantanamo on the first day he was in office. As I write this he has been enthroned for over 2,000 days and this mockery of justice and due process remains open.

• El Presidente has overseen the "Pivot to Asia," thereby ratcheting up tensions in the Pacific, and further lining the already diamond-studded pockets of the Military Industrial Cyst.

• He has continued to encircle Russia with NATO bases in direct violation of agreements reached with them after the fall of the Berlin Wall.

• President Obama has one-upped his recent Oval Office predecessors by secretly overthrowing the democratically elected government of the Ukraine. (This is not a secret to those who get their information from the alternative media.) He has installed a puppet regime there to do the West's bidding. This particular strategic blunder is extraordinary because of the sheer lack of prior research about which group of "freedom fighters" they were backing this time. The U.S. has a long history of supporting vicious, genocidal dictators. Indeed, the operative phrase has long seemed to be, "Yes, he is a ruthless tyrant—but he is *our* ruthless tyrant." Well, in this obscene instance they have managed to either knowingly or unknowingly find themselves a band of swastika-wearing neo-Nazis to "spread democracy."

• His administration continues to destabilize any government whose resources or strategic position could be valuable to American Global Capitalists. Libya and Syria and Egypt are the most recent examples of this divide-and-conquer tactic.

• He did nothing to end or lessen the latest Israeli butchery in Gaza. And he looks the other way when the Zionists grab more of the West Bank.

• Instead of denouncing the planet-wide electronic surveillance carried out by the NSA on both enemies and allies, the President is an apologist for such despicable conduct. If it serves the bankers or corporations or the military, it is okay with him.

• He has prosecuted more whistleblowers than any president in the last... well, actually... more than all the previous presidents combined.

• He has established an imperial beachhead in Africa by instituting AfriCom. So who knows how many poor African countries our Special Forces are now clandestinely destabilizing under the cloak and dagger banner of JSOC? Check out Jeremy Scahill's brilliant reporting on this topic.

• And saving the best for last, he has become President God. Every Tuesday he pontificates on who should be "neutralized" by drone strikes based on intelligence from agencies who are wrong so frequently that their efforts would be considered comedic if they weren't so tragic. And since His Omnipotence is protecting "national security," what does it matter if the collateral damage splatters women and children all over the roadside?

So, let me see—that's *ten* bullet points that instantly sprang to mind without even having to do a Google search. Just one of these should immediately disqualify a person for consideration by the selectors in Norway. (Yes, not Sweden. For some myste-

rious reason the Nobel will mandates that a committee of par-
liamentarians in Norway choose the Peace Prize winner.) How
these judges continually ignore the most significant impedi-
ment to world peace just astonishes me. Are they really a
panel of Norwegians—or a clan of super-patriotic Nebraskans?
Assuming that they are not malevolent but simply misguided,
let me remind them of why U.S. foreign policy is justifiably
scorned by most of the planet.

• The U.S. now has over 800 military bases blanketing almost
the entire planet. These forces are not stationed there to protect the local population. Their role is to enforce the will of the
American multinational corporations who bleed the cheap resources or slave labor from these nations. These installations
also siphon enormous wealth to the Military-Industrial Cyst.
• The U.S. continues to spy on... well, essentially everyone
that their advanced technology allows them to spy on. Their
excuse is that they are protecting us from terrorism, but it is
common world-wide knowledge that the CIA and the Pentagon
fund, arm, train and unleash large numbers of terrorists. The
only difference is that these groups are designated by the cap-
tive mainstream media as "freedom fighters."
• One of the main operating principles of modern U.S. foreign policy is the Wolfowitz Doctrine. This decree calls for the
use of whatever tactics are necessary to keep another nation
(think China and Russia) from becoming strong enough to
threaten America's domination of the world.
• Since World War II the United States has attempted to
overthrow 50 governments—most of them democratically
elected; attempted to assassinate more than 50 foreign leaders
(some of them—such as Fidel Castro—multiple times); attempted to suppress populist or nationalist movements in 20
countries; and dropped bombs on the people of 30 countries.
• Unsatisfied with just ruling the planet, American political
and military elites have now adopted a policy of "full spectrum

dominance." This means that they also want to dominate outer space and cyberspace as theaters of war.

And so, for you selectors in Norway, struggling to regain some relevancy for your Peace Prize, hopefully this will clarify for you what an 800-pound War Lord standing in the middle of Planet Earth's living room looks like. And now, to assist you even further in regaining some respect for your extremely tarnished award, let me suggest some very worthy candidates.

If I had the financial ability to designate a Sea Gypsy Philosopher Peace Prize, these would be some of the individuals on my short list. I would be delighted if the Nobel Committee would research some of these gallant Warriors of the Pen, who have dedicated their lives to unmasking the true, evil face of U.S. foreign policy. Here they are:

• Daniel Ellsberg... This whistleblower who released the Pentagon Papers had a profound influence on winding down the senseless and obscene Vietnam War. He even suffered prison time as a result of this courageous act of conscience. He has continued ever since to battle the American War Machine. Here is one of his insightful quotes about Vietnam: "It wasn't that we were *on* the wrong side, we *were* the wrong side!"

• Oliver Stone... When this man crafts a brilliant anti-war movie such as *Platoon*, he knows of what he speaks. As an idealistic but foolish young man he went off to Vietnam to help protect democracy and got a profound lesson about the true nature of war, in particular its senseless lunacy. He was wounded both physically and emotionally. But he has converted those scars into a body of cinematic art that reveals more about the true nature of power than probably any other director. And he continues to use his art to bring more light into a world deliberately cloaked in darkness and doubt. His TV show "The Untold History of the United States" brilliantly exposes the vast and profound difference between what leaders tell us they are doing and what they are actually perpetrating—and I use the word "perp" deliberately.

• Cindy Sheehan... When she lost her son in the Iraq War II, she had the courage to ask the question which so many other parents of dead soldiers only voiced to themselves: "What did he die for?" Since his death, she has devoted her life to anti-war activism using a variety of approaches, from running for office to her most daring campaign, during which she pitched her tent and lived in protest near President Bush's Texas vacation compound, which became known as Camp Casey in honor of her dead son. She has been arrested time and time again as she continues to throw herself on the gears of the American War Machine.

• John Pilger... This Australian, who has spent much of his life revealing the filthy underbelly of Empire and Globalization, is an investigative journalist and brilliant documentary filmmaker. In his very first film he shocked the world by revealing that U.S. troops in Vietnam had so deeply lost their belief in the war that many of them were turning mutinous. That was the first exposé in a lifetime of fine work unveiling the true motives of those in power as they plunder the planet.

• William Blum... This tireless campaigner, who looks like everyone's harmless uncle from Syracuse, has actually been a valiant superhero when it comes to shining light on the dark secrets of U.S. overseas malignancy. His books document with incredible thoroughness the atrocities that those behind the American Throne have been visiting on the world. But besides being encyclopedic, they are also riveting reading. Such scholarship combined with literary flair is a rare combination.

There are many other peace campaigners who I deeply admire and who deserve consideration from the judges in Oslo. I will be glad to steer them towards these individuals, and in this regard my email address is right here: seagypsyphilosopher@gmail.com (Naturally, I realize that they will never contact me, and will probably never even see this essay.)

But unlike the fool's valor of Don Quixote who flailed away with his fractured lance at imaginary demons, our adversaries are very real and deserve the scorn of all persons of good will. These people, who are so pathologically addicted to domination that they want to rule the world, must be stymied and defeated. And awarding a prestigious Peace Prize to heroes who actually crusade for Peace will certainly help in this often hopeless but eternally noble quest.

Homage to My Wonderful Mom

*T*HE MELANCHOLY is heavy on me this morning. It is my mom's death day. And even though it was on a September 5th many years ago, I still grieve... deeply. I was beside her in the emergency room in her final minutes. She was already unconscious and the doctors were trying to shock her back. I knew she would not return. She had told me so the day before.

* * *

It had been her first day of physical therapy after a very severe cardiac attack that left her with only a third of a functioning heart. With me holding one arm and the nurse on the other, we tried to gently help her take a few steps. She could not. This just staggered her. When the nurse left us alone we had our last conversation together.

I tried to encourage her by emphasizing that the progress back to mobility would be slow, but that it would come. And I emphasized that her five children would be able to take turns visiting and encouraging her in her recovery. My message was that even though her body was weak, her will was strong, and she could regain a satisfying and meaningful life. But she felt—

and her instinct was probably correct—that the best she could expect was the slavery of a wheelchair and a grim future in an assisted care facility, watching TV with a bunch of other sad invalids.

She did not want to burden her children with the monetary expense that such an existence would involve. And she was emphatic about not wishing to end her days as a sickly and dependent woman. So she confessed that when the next heart attack came, she would "let it take her." And she drew me close and whispered to me in words far more poetic than I could ever write, "My wonderful first born child, there is a time for fighting and a time for farewell. I've been able to say my goodbyes to all of you kids now. The love and affection that you blessed me with here in the hospital has been so beautiful and so comforting that I am... ready."

Such wisdom and eloquence was so overwhelming, that all I could do was hug her gently... and cry... as I am doing now.

* * *

My mom totally devoted her life to her children. And she was overjoyed by how we turned out. I too, am proud of what fine, caring and joyful people my brother and sisters are. And we all realize that most of our best qualities stem from her selfless nurturing.

Even though she only had a high school education, her understanding of the joy and sorrow of human existence far exceeded what I learned from my college philosophy professors. Of all the lessons that she imparted to me, the most important was the need for basic human decency. And she knew that the compass that leads an individual to such enlightened moral conduct is within all of us. She understood that we do not need governmental regulations or religious dogma to teach us how to behave towards one another. She emphasized that such knowledge is a part of everyone's core wisdom.

Mom was also very courageous. My dad was a scientist—a smart and successful organic chemist with many patents to his credit. He wanted me, as the first-born male child, to follow in his footsteps. But I was always drawn to the arts. The words of Socrates and Shakespeare sang to me, but chemistry did not. This led to intense emotional turmoil at a very formative stage of my life. My mother would always defend me, and encouraged me to do whatever I wished in life as long as it harmed no one else.

My contrary-to-ordinary spirit must have certainly tested her patience in this regard, but she never complained. For example, I clearly expressed my rebelliousness during my senior year at college. I had been elected president of my student body. For the yearbook photo, my cabinet all wore standard coats and ties, but I dressed like Steve McQueen playing a lumberjack. When I showed it to her she laughed until she cried and then she hugged me tightly and said, "You just keep being yourself, son. Don't ever worry about them!"

* * *

Even when I returned from Vietnam and turned my back on my college education and became a San Francisco street performer, she never wavered in her support and encouragement. One episode from that period is amongst my most cherished memories. After 10 years as a prominent street juggler, the Mayor of San Francisco honored me with an official "Ray Jason Day." The award was to be presented at a large event with thousands of people in attendance. I flew my mom out for the celebration. As the Mayor finished her speech and handed me the ornate certificate, my mom leapt to her feet and started applauding with her hands above her head, no less. The rest of the audience immediately joined her and for a fleeting moment in a sweet, rich life, I knew what it felt like to be a folk hero.

On that same visit, we went on a road trip. During my childhood, my mom chose Spanish names for all of our family dogs —Pedro, Jose and Pancho. I was too young to detect how odd this was. She also had a proclivity towards cheap Mexican statuary that she used as yard decorations. In her defense, she never went so low-brow as to buy a *muchacho* in a sombrero leaning against a cactus.

But as her kids grew up, we did razz her about this in a good-natured way. Eventually, I assumed that she must have had a brief fling with a handsome Mexican before she met my dad. But she had never actually been to Mexico—and so off we went. For her very first night south of the border, I had chosen a hotel that used to be favored by movie stars. I believe it is called the Rosario Beach Resort. Upon our arrival it was definitely not as glamorous as it had been when Clark Gable might have visited.

But it was more than good enough for us. Sitting on the restaurant veranda drinking margaritas and watching the sun slide into the Pacific, we clinked our glasses together and shared a glance that was a blend of both joy and sadness. For it certainly seemed at that moment that this might be as close as human beings can ever approach true happiness.

* * *

When I sailed away from the San Francisco street performing scene to become a full-time sea gypsy, she again was a beacon of encouragement. She especially liked the fact that I was helping to pay for my wanderings by writing for the sailing magazines. She loved being able to go to the grocery store and pick up an issue with one of my stories in it. I have no doubt that she enthusiastically pointed out my article to the bored, teenage check-out clerk who couldn't care less.

But she loved it even more when I would visit her in person and regale her with my silly tales. On one of my visits we went to a Fourth of July fireworks show at the nearby fairgrounds. The spectacle started uneventfully with the usual oohs and aahs on the really good ones. Suddenly, a rocket that should have soared 200 feet into the air exploded after climbing only about 20 feet. The workers feeding the cannons immediately knew it was a dud and dove for cover. Their dark silhouettes as they lunged for safety were perfectly freeze-framed by the exploding fireworks.

Through the rest of the show about every fifth rocket was a dud, and the poor pyrotechnicians had to catapult themselves out of harm's way. My mom dubbed it the Three Stooges Fireworks Show. Even in her final days, we laughed joyously when we recalled that distant summer evening.

* * *

After our mother died, my sister Cindy was kind enough to go through mom's belongings. She found a card that mom had set aside for my 50th birthday. Even from the grave she was encouraging me to remain faithful to my own Path. It reads:

"Always be true to yourself, my son, for there is greatness within you!"

Beneath the text there is a watercolor painting of two sailboats gliding side by side. Even though I am a single-hander, whenever I am out there, I like to think that I am not alone and that my mom is back there sailing a watchful parallel course on that other boat.

Postscript: My mom never got to read my first book, *Tales Of A Sea Gypsy*, so she didn't get to see my heartfelt dedication.

For My Mom

She abandoned her own wanderlust
in order to dedicate her life to her five children.
That nurturing sacrifice allowed
my gypsy spirit to soar.
In hundreds of ports and half a hundred
countries, her quiet lessons
of compassion, humor and courage
have smoothed this vagabond's path.

Reality TV is Unreal

*M*Y FRIEND Dmitry Orlov, who shares my belief that sailing boats are both excellent living platforms and superb escape modules, sent me an interesting email a few days ago. He had been contacted by a stranger who was interested in possibly featuring him in a Reality TV show about "larger-than-life self-reliant sailors." Dmitry gracefully deflected that overture, and put him in touch with me instead.

Coincidentally, I had been sorting through my notes on possible future essay topics, and was focusing in on an anti-television message. This well-intentioned man's email proved to be an excellent catalyst for my thoughts on this rarely-examined cornerstone of the modern world. This is the exact email letter that I sent to him with the exception that I have changed his name—to protect the innocent...

1 June 14
Hello Brandon,
Thanks for getting in touch with me. I suspect that your motive was benevolent; and that you are generously trying to help people become new Reality TV stars.

As Dmitry mentioned, I am quite expert on the topic of ocean-going sailboats as sustainable living modules and as ideal survival platforms in the case of a societal collapse. He and I are probably the leading thinkers on this topic. That is the *good* news. But there is some significant and overriding *bad* news.

I believe that television is profoundly harmful to society. And I find Reality TV repellent.

Such strong words shout out for substantiation, so allow me to do so. First, let me address television in general. I could go to one of the "alternative bibles" that I keep in my ship's library, which is Jerry Mander's *Four Arguments For The Elimination Of Television*, and spend a day re-reading it and then respond to you. But instead, I will just list a few of the troublesome aspects of television that spring immediately to mind:

• Television accelerates Humanity's divorce from Nature. Seeing an orca whale on the tube is not even close to experiencing it from a small boat in the wilderness.

• TV is a far more powerful communication medium than print sources. Its deliberately manipulated imagery is so strong that it almost "sears" itself into the brain. For example, notice how difficult it is to remove vapid advertising jingles from your head decades after you last heard them.

• Television malevolently sanitizes imagery of the most horrible aspects of human behavior. If the actual footage of dismembered, smoking bodies of children in war zones was displayed on TV, it would soon put war profiteers out of business. Yet we never see that type of coverage because the warmongers are also significant television advertisers, and they call the shots.

• TV contributes significantly to the obesity epidemic. Hours that in my youth were spent outdoors playing and burning calories are now replaced with couch time for most kids.

• Television greatly serves the interests of the ruling elites, since only they can afford to buy significant air time to promote their electoral candidates or oppose ballot propositions. And with the concentration of media giants currently in place, it means that six mega-corporations control the vast majority of what is communicated to people.

• The tube attacks diversity in the world. It homogenizes society and leads to a global monoculture.

• Television is the enemy of truth. Advertising is all about fraud and deceit. The deadly consequences of cigarette smoking were camouflaged for decades on TV. And now, the toxicity of our processed food "products" is being deliberately hidden from us.

• TV separates us from each other. The "conversation around the family dinner table" is now considered a quaint relic of bygone times.

• The tube does not make us the "best informed citizens in history." The information we receive is rarely meaningful or provocative or in any way challenging to the status quo. And the flow is so vast and overpowering that there is no chance to reflect on it. Yes, you can get water from a fire hose, but it is extremely difficult to drink from it at that speed and volume.

• Television is stalking you. Just "turning it off" is nearly impossible since it is almost everywhere—bars, dental offices, gyms, airports and on and on, but not off and off!

Now let me deal specifically with the phenomenon of Reality TV, and the damaging ways that it impacts our society:

• Reality TV is to reality what Velveeta is to cheese. During my decades as a professional entertainer, I sometimes had television crews follow me around for days at a time in order to do what were termed "up close and personal" profiles in those days. Having a camera lens around undeniably affects the daily dynamic. It is distortion and not reality.

• Reality TV glorifies competition and marginalizes cooperation. And even when cooperation is utilized, it is often just a tactic to outmaneuver someone so that they get "voted off the island."

• In a world already too fixated with celebrity worship, how can it be beneficial to society to glorify pawn shop clerks with a TV show?

• Reality shows reinforce the myth that acquiring fame and fortune should be everyone's primary life goals. It glorifies rampant materialism and better-than-thou status seeking.

I hope that this letter has not been upsetting to you. Wait a minute... that's not true at all. In fact, I hope that it has jolted your perception of this enormously powerful cultural force that we take for granted and almost never examine. I realize that my contrarian views are in the tiny minority; and for every objector like myself, there are 1,000 people craving a shot at Reality TV. For them it is the road to fame. But for me, it would be the road to shame.

Sincerely,

Ray Jason

Mutually Assured Incineration

*I*T WAS HALFWAY between midnight and dawn, and the moon had summoned me. As an ocean sailor who has navigated my lovely boat across the wide waters using just the stars and my sextant, I pay more attention to the sky than city-folk. And I also pay more attention to the Earth than many sailor-folk.

At this very instant there are at least 150 blue water sail-boats within 10 miles of me. Their crews sleep peacefully. They are not wondering, like I am, whether this lunar oddity will be the final one that humanity witnesses. For tonight's full moon will be the last one that falls on a Friday the 13th until 2049. The question that troubles me is this: "Will the human project still exist in 35 years?" My concern is not just delusional pessimism. It is mushroom cloud terror.

I recently learned of potentially apocalyptic policy changes that the U.S. government has made to its nuclear war strategic planning. These radical and malevolent alterations were never debated by the people's representatives in Congress. Nor were they revealed to the citizens themselves for community discussion. And op-ed columns did not appear in the mainstream press critiquing such lunatic fantasies. Instead, these Dr. Strangelove plans were made in secrecy—and for good reason

—since any decent human being who is not metastasized by their own lust for power would never even consider such hideous war-planning.

* * *

During the Cold War, the government mindset was that nuclear weapons would only be used in retaliation should another party use them first. The operative phrase that defined this policy was "Mutually Assured Destruction." The rationale was that since both the U.S. and the Soviet Union each possessed enough nukes to destroy each other many times over, neither nation would attempt a "first strike." The aggressor in such a situation understood that the missiles they launched would result in a counter-attack that would vaporize their cities and convert their continent into a toxic moonscape.

During the 1980s, Ronald Reagan jeopardized this delicate and vital balance by promoting the Strategic Defense Initiative, which the media dubbed "Star Wars." This was an attempt to create a nuclear shield whereby sophisticated missiles could intercept any Soviet rockets headed for the USA. The goals of such a project were obvious to the Soviet military: The U.S. could launch a first strike and feel confident that most of the Soviet counter-attack would be destroyed by the Star Wars protective dome.

Fortunately, this ABM (Anti-Ballistic Missile) system failed miserably while still in its early test stages. The contractors behind the scheme had essentially conned Reagan with radioactive pie-in-the-sky deceptions. This failure meant that Soviet citizens could rest easier. The whole world should have been able to rest easier a few years later in 1989 when the entire Soviet Union collapsed. This was the perfect opportunity to dismantle and destroy every nuclear weapon on the planet.

But the arms makers were not about to let that happen. No matter how many million signatures soccer moms accumulated on disarmament petitions, the war profiteers would not surrender. Just because they were already grotesquely rich should not deter them from becoming obscenely rich.

* * *

A turning point in the attitude of U.S. decision makers towards nuclear weapons was quietly marked in the spring of 2006 when *Foreign Affairs* magazine published a crucial article entitled "The Rise of U.S. Nuclear Primacy." This publication, which most Americans have never even heard of, is extremely influential in the halls of power—although in this case I might more appropriately term them "the bunkers of power." The authors argued persuasively that both the Russians and the Chinese had fallen far behind the U.S. in their ability to go *mano a mano* (that is, missile-to-missile) in a nuclear exchange.

In the eight years since that article appeared, the superiority gap has widened even more dramatically. To further jeopardize the fragile stalemate that had existed for decades, the Neo-conservatives, who designed the Bush II foreign policy and who are also prominent in the Obama White House, have bundled almost all of the former Soviet countries under the NATO banner. The purported reason? To "spread democracy," but their true purpose was to position military installations in countries which are geographically close to Russia. This further weakens the Kremlin's ability to retaliate should a first-strike nuke attack be unleashed against them.

Amongst the complexities of the present crisis in the Ukraine, the American mainstream media never even mentions that Putin understands the extreme danger of having advanced ABM launchers in an adjoining country. Reverse the situation and imagine how the U.S. would react if Russia positioned such weapons in Vancouver, Toronto and Halifax.

To aggravate a dangerous situation even more, the U.S. government is no longer even claiming that our nuclear armaments are for deterrence only. The latest official statement on this, called the 2013 Nuclear Employment Strategy, reads in part:

"The 2010 Nuclear Posture Review established the Administration's goal to set conditions that would allow the United States to safely adopt a policy of making deterrence of nuclear attack the sole purpose of U.S. nuclear weapons. Although we cannot adopt such a policy today, the new guidance reiterates the intention to work towards that goal over time."

But if we already have a significant advantage over the other nuclear powers, and if we have so many emergencies crying out for attention at home—such as massive unemployment and a decaying infrastructure—certainly we would not waste money on more nuclear firepower. Actually, we would: On January 8, 2014, Defense Secretary Chuck Hagel announced what Reuters termed "ambitious plans to upgrade U.S. nuclear weapons systems by modernizing weapons and building new submarines, missiles and bombers to deliver them." Apparently our 7,700 nuclear weapons are not sufficient, but this additional hardware, at a price tag of anywhere between 355 billion and one *trillion* dollars, will finally do the trick of keeping us secure.

* * *

Which brings me to an obvious question: What is this *really* all about? When the Berlin Wall came down and the Cold War ended, I can understand keeping NATO in existence for a few years to make sure that Russia did not have some secret aggressive strategy planned. But it has been 25 years now. Why does NATO even still exist?

I believe that it lingers because it is a more subtle way to impose American hegemony on the rest of the planet. And to save everyone the trouble of racing to the dictionary to look up the H word, let me phrase it more simply—the U.S. wants to rule the world. The average American does not want to do so, but those in power seem to salivate for that sort of control. They use the phrases "American exceptionalism" and the "indispensable nation" and "spreading democracy" as camouflage for the most blatant and vicious acts of aggression. The last 50 years of world history have been dominated by the U.S. corporate and military interests imposing their will on the rest of the planet. (Check out William Blum's book *Rogue State* for a shockingly detailed inventory of this cavalcade of evil.) If sacks of money wouldn't do the trick, then in would come the assassins and then the bombers and now the drones.

But let me return to the question I asked two paragraphs ago. "What is this *really* all about?" Any honest observer who pays attention to American deeds rather than to its rhetoric can clearly see that the U.S. is essentially an out-of-control imperialist bully. As hideous as that is, it is not shocking. That's because the history of "civilization" is a record of one vicious tyrant after another ascending to power and conquering other lands and populations. And as disgusting as *that* is, at least there was a motive, since it involved the theft of land or resources or slaves. But to launch an all-out nuclear attack where there would be no "spoils of war" is what I refer to as "EBC Syndrome": Evil Beyond Comprehension. Let me delve into this malignant pathology more deeply:

• **Show me the enemy!** Neither Russia nor China has declared war against the U.S.—nor have they indicated an aggressive posture towards America. On the contrary, they both have shown a total willingness to peacefully coexist with the West. This is the perfect historical opportunity to *eliminate* the threat of nuclear annihilation from the planet. But by increasing and upgrading its already obese stockpile of these weapons, Washington is forcing these other countries to do the same, practically demanding a new arms race. As an example of this, look around the web and you will discover that hypersonic delivery systems that travel at 10 times the speed of sound are now being developed.

• **Describe a nuclear "victory."** Perhaps our "leaders," are trapped in some time bubble where they imagine that modern nuclear war will resemble Hiroshima, and that a few weeks after the attack it will be safe to return to the incinerated areas. It's as if they have visions of Halliburton and KBR and Bechtel trucks caravanning East to build a new Eurasian-America. Ah, yes—Disney Siberia! But the current nuclear warheads are so much stronger and more devastating. Any scientist who has studied their impacts concludes that with the poisoned water and radioactive soil, human life will be impossible there for a *very* long time.

• **Let's destroy ourselves.** Given the insanity of attacking "non-enemies" and killing them all and rendering their lands uninhabitable, what is the possible motivation? All I can come up with is that maybe these monsters are willing to convert half the planet's landmass into a lifeless lava field because it will eliminate any threats to their power. But if they are Machiavellian enough to plot such diabolical lunacy, how can their think tanks not anticipate the wider consequences? Spend an hour reading the research that Steven Starr summarizes at his website, www.nucleardarkness.org, and it will be obvious that only the cockroaches are winners in a nuclear war. Firestorms would become so immense that a blanket of smoke would enshroud the planet in darkness, thus eliminating any food growing since freezing temperatures would occur every day for years. Everyone who didn't have their skin peeled off their body instantly, or die of radiation poisoning some time later, would die of starvation not very long after that.

• **The core reality.** In my opinion what is really driving this aberrant suicidal behavior is this: a relatively small group of men, who already have too much wealth and too much power, are insatiably lusting after even more wealth and greater power. Their behavior is psychotic and pathological and genocidal. We must stop electing and appointing them. We must start institutionalizing them.

* * *

After watching that Friday the 13th full moon descend behind the mountain to the west of me, I remained on *Aventura*'s deck, searching for an insight that I sensed was lurking just beneath the surface of my reason. And then it gently eased up into my consciousness. Here is that message:

I believe that there are only two ways in which humanity can actually destroy itself. One is nuclear annihilation and the other is through catastrophic climate change. But if governments could sincerely embrace the One Human Family concept, and eradicate all nuclear weapons from the Earth, we could then dedicate the immense financial resources currently spent on them to a global crusade to minimize the onrushing climate change tsunami. Such a worldwide campaign to change the human paradigm in an overwhelmingly positive manner might ripple out and create a much wider renaissance.

People might start valuing cooperation more than competition. Neighbors might cherish diversity instead of fearing it. Friendship and family and community might become more desired than "stuff." And to make such a movement a little less abstract and a little more tangible, allow me to suggest a name for it. Let's call it The Reversing Course Initiative.

Suicidal Growth

*S*AILING DOWN the decades, my sweet little boat and I have witnessed some amazing meteor showers while alone at sea. During those nights I always listen to Debussy's lyrical masterpiece "Reverie" while lying on my back and marveling at the falling stars. And what makes it even more sublime is being the only human presence in that sector of the planet. It reminds me of how utterly tiny Homo sapiens is in the grand scheme of things. Unfortunately, back on land the dominant perspective is just the opposite. Humanity considers itself the grand actor in the center of the cosmic stage, and nature is merely the backdrop.

But my almost visceral understanding of just how minuscule our species is inspires me to view our human project in a radically different manner. Spend as much time alone at sea as I have, and you too might find yourself transformed from being an Accepter to a Questioner. In this essay I will discuss a topic that is almost universally embraced and yet never challenged. That subject is growth. How can somebody argue against growth, you might wonder? Well, hopefully I can do so calmly and convincingly.

* * *

Even a sixth-grader understands that infinite growth on a finite planet is impossible. This is not an "economic issue" to be debated; it is an ecological fact that must be addressed. Our planet has limited resources and our survival hinges upon our ability to allocate and preserve them. The two great enemies of sustainability on Earth are runaway population growth and conspicuous consumption growth. Together they are a recipe for biological botulism.

Population overshoot has been fervently debated ever since Thomas Malthus first introduced it back in 1798. In the 1960s, Paul and Anne Ehrlich reignited the discussion with their cautionary book *The Population Bomb*. The timeline of their predictions did not come true, because they had not foreseen the Green Revolution that massively expanded industrial agriculture. But now food output *has* peaked while population expansion continues to accelerate. So a significant population decrease is essential.

But there is a huge force in the world which will not allow this to happen: Big Religion. The major monotheistic churches want their membership to grow as enormously and rapidly as possible. But they never admit to such selfish motives. Instead, they claim that they are merely following god's edict that birth control shall be forbidden and that the flock shall go forth and multiply.

If you doubt the truth of this indictment, consider this. If the Catholic Church injunction against birth control is not just designed to increase their enrollment, then they will not object to this suggestion: let every other child that is born to a Catholic parent be raised as a Muslim. Observe how the church fathers respond to that recommendation, and you will quickly understand that their birth tyranny edicts are not about god's will, but are instead about increasing their membership and their power.

Another more subtle impact of Big Religion's dictatorial population stance is how it affects education. There is a direct link between a higher level of education and a lower birth rate. The least-educated segments of society tend to be the most religious, and so women who are forbidden by the church to use birth control devices soon become "birth increase" devices. Since they are burdened with almost constant childbirth, they have little time for education or for the widening of their personal horizons and opportunities. They become slaves to reproduction and to Big Religion.

But one thing that I can't emphasize enough is the fact that this issue does not even get discussed in any meaningful way. If you think that bringing up politics and religion is a sure way to derail a conversation in polite company, just interject the issue of population control and notice how almost everyone considers it a taboo subject. And yet overpopulation is a major element—if not *the* major factor—in the history of every single civilization that has collapsed.

* * *

The second type of growth that is so hazardous to our planet and all of its creatures is our lust for stuff. Although the USA is largely innocent when it comes to causing population problems, it is unmistakably guilty when it comes to promoting rampant consumerism. The American Way of Life is worshipped and imitated around the globe. Through its movies and television and product saturation, the American Empire spreads its own religion with missionary zeal—The Church of the Mall. The message of that gospel is that happiness is achieved by owning things. The corollary to this is that more stuff equals more fulfillment. Embracing such a vapid worldview has dire consequences for the Individual, the Society and the Planet.

For people, it means that values such as the affection of friends, the solidarity of community, and the appreciation of beauty are all subordinate to the less-meaningful and often-endless craving for more stuff. I contend that the world is not better off with cars that talk to us or 671 types of "yogurt products" or phones so expensive that one has to take out a loan to purchase them.

Many of my sea gypsy years have been spent in countries that are referred to as "Third World." (The modern, polite-yet-insulting term is "Developing World.") I have carefully observed that there is an inverse relationship between personal happiness and owning a lot of things: Only 30 yards from where I am now typing, I will often marvel at Indio children playing joyously for hours with just a coconut and a stick. And yet just down the dock, First World kids will be miserable because their electronic game console is not the latest version.

Aside from the damage that insatiable consumption inflicts on the individual, it also has extremely harmful consequences for the larger society. When a person fixates on buying more things and interfacing with more machines, they forget to exercise their power of critical thinking. They are so mesmerized and distracted by the latest iEverything that they don't even notice their slide into consumer slavery. A society with a colossal wealth discrepancy between the rich and the poor, with meaningless work that is numbing and degrading, all watched over by a tyrannical police/surveillance grid, should be cause for code-red alarm. But instead, most people barely notice it because there is an enormous plasma TV in the way.

But our addiction to more and more stuff is not just harmful to individuals and to societies. It is utterly catastrophic to our one and only life-supporting planet. Our constant-growth consumerism pollutes the air, decimates the ocean's fish stocks, poisons the rivers, and blows away the topsoil.

* * *

This combo platter of increasing population growth and unceasing consumer growth is a recipe for societal suicide. Too many people and too much stuff are ravaging all of the support systems that keep us alive. We need breathable air, drinkable water, fertile land, plus renewable and non-renewable resources. But we are decreasing all of these vital necessities and at the same time we are increasing all of the waste products that our excesses are generating. This cannot end well! But it *can* end horribly!

P.S. For excellent information on how to steadily decrease population without coercion, visit Bill Ryerson's site populationmedia.org. He has nobly dedicated 40 years of his life to this unpopular cause.

94

An Anti-War Lamentation

I AM ROWING HOME to my boat, which is anchored in a beautiful, isolated cove near Key West. Suddenly, the solitude and peacefulness is shattered by the sound of two military jets shrieking back towards the nearby airbase.

As I cover my ears and look scornfully towards them, a sport fishing boat comes blasting out of the mangroves with 500 horsepower ensnared in its outboard motors. I wonder to myself if the fish that they will catch in their $100,000 boat will taste any better than the one that I just speared from my little rowboat.

When they pass beside me and see me covering my ears, they holler over to me, "That's the sound of freedom." I nod noncommittally. For the remainder of the day my mind could not stop thinking about what I wish I could have said to them. If only we could have shared a beer and some grilled fish and some open-mindedness, I would have tried to give them a different perspective on the true essence of that sound.

* * *

In America, and in fact in most of the world, we do not realize how thoroughly we have been manipulated by The Malignant Overlords. These are the politicians, the religious leaders, the media owners, and the corporate tycoons who shape our way of looking at the world. This "sound of freedom" myth is a perfect example of how they exploit us. And even more sadly and tragically, it is a grim reminder of how we accept their deceptions without even questioning their truthfulness.

In the U.S. we have never been under siege. We have never known the wrath of outside invaders, whether they were on horseback, in tanks or in supersonic aircraft. Our towns have never been bombed, our children killed and our wives and sisters raped. But much of the world has experienced this. And in some places they have repeatedly suffered this grotesque horror down through the centuries.

When we hear the roar of a combat jet overhead, it is just an aircraft that is practicing for a mission far, far away. Many of us would look skyward and be proud of the young "Top Gun" pilot who is protecting our way of life. The fierce noise that it makes is merely a minor nuisance in our daily lives, and it presents no danger to us whatsoever. So most Americans tolerate it, because it is supposedly "the sound of freedom."

* * *

But for a mother far, far away, the sound of a jet means something entirely different—something insanely horrible and senseless. That evil supersonic dragon screeching in from the horizon could transform her beautiful daughter, full of life and laughter, into a pulp of bloody, burning flesh. It means that the putrid smell of her charred, dying child and the anguished sound of the little girl's screams and whimpers as she yearns for the release of death will remain with that mom for the rest of her tortured days.

Are those jets the "sound of freedom" for that mom? Is the horrific pestilence that they spew from the sky acceptable because they are "spreading democracy?" The great peace pilgrim Mahatma Gandhi answered those questions about a half a century ago when he wrote, "What difference does it make to the dead, the orphans and the homeless, whether the mad destruction is wrought under the name of totalitarianism or the holy name of liberty or democracy?"

To a mom with a murdered child in her arms it makes no difference. And it makes no sense. Should one ever kill innocents because some people believe that their political system is better than the political system of some other people? If you are inclined to answer "yes" to that question then I suggest that you reverse the situation: If The Malignant Overlords of some other country sent their jets into your skies to bomb you into adopting their political system would you find that acceptable? No, you would not. And yet you permit your own government to do just that!

But what is even worse is the fact that the true motivation for sending in the bombers probably had very little to do with spreading democracy and a whole lot to do with capturing territory or gaining control of some valuable natural resource. Somewhere, deep within that mourning mother, there is probably the realization that this whole nightmare is an accident of geography. If her family lived in a place that did not have oil flowing beneath the ground there would be no attack, there would be no mutilation, and there would be no everlasting yearning for her lost child.

* * *

Another pair of jets just screamed by, and this time I actually curse them as I sit in the cockpit of my boat filleting the fish that I caught for my dinner. I have been trying to climb inside the head of the tormented mother with her dead daughter in her arms, and imagine what she thinks of the pilot of that despicable plane.

Does she wonder how he could be smart enough to fly one of those complicated machines and yet too dumb to realize the true consequences of his actions? Does she question whether he has ever had to actually witness the severed bones, the spewing guts and the smoking hair of his victims? Does she believe that he is not a hero but a coward, since he rains this murderous horror from the sky and yet is rarely in any danger of being shot down himself due to the superiority of his technology?

Does she suspect that he has been so warped by an adolescence spent in front of violent video games that he can no longer distinguish between actual carnage and electronic destruction? Does she cringe when she realizes that by spreading lifelong misery he is a hero in his homeland and is guaranteed a high-paying airline job when his military days are over?

Does she think any or all of these things? Or can she only think of the limp, little body in her arms, and her daughter's wasted, exterminated future? When she hears the echo of that jet down the tormented decades of her life, will she hear the sound of freedom... or will she hear the sound of butchery?

Dear Nobel Prize
for Economics Committee

*I*T WAS NAUTICAL SWAP MEET day in my quiet corner of the southwest Caribbean. Sailboats were arriving from all over the archipelago to buy, sell, trade or give things away. We affectionately refer to the goods as "treasures of the bilge" but many of the items could just as easily be described as "donations for the dumpster." The event, which takes place every couple of months, is not just about commerce—it is also about friendship. Many people attend with the primary intention of just visiting with their sea gypsy pals from the far shores of our little inland sea.

I love these events—not just for the camaraderie—but because they are proof positive that economic activity does *not* have to be convoluted and incomprehensible. It can be honest and fair and beneficial. This face-to-face, no-middleman type of commerce is such an abnormality in our world that it got me pondering the nature and purpose of modern economics. In order to make this complex topic more understandable, I decided to frame this essay as an open letter to the Nobel Prize for Economics Committee.

Before getting into my actual communiqué to the jurors, the back-story of the award itself should be shared with you. Alfred Nobel did not establish a Nobel Prize for Economics. The fields of human endeavor that he wished to applaud and encourage were Peace, Literature, Medicine, Physics and Chemistry. The award for economics is an "add-on." Its formal name is The Sveriges Riksbank Prize in Economic Sciences in Memory of Alfred Nobel. And guess what the Sveriges Riksbank is? If you answered "the Swedish Central Bank" then you passed your Econ pop quiz.

Now, a skeptic might contend that this award is riding on the coattails of the Nobel Prize reputation. And a cynic might add that the glorified phrase "Economic Sciences" indicates profound self-doubt as to the genuine merit of this field of study. A quick glance at the 2013 prize tarnishes the image of this prestigious award even further. The committee described it in this language: "The recipients were honored for their empirical analysis of asset prices." But amazingly, two of the 2013 laureates have completely opposing theories on asset prices. It is like awarding the physics prize to someone who argues that gravity forces objects downwards and then sharing that award with a scientist claiming that gravity propels them upwards.

In the world of common sense this is absurd, but in the kingdom of academia it appears to be meritorious. It certainly seems like the goal of many scientists and academics is not to simplify and clarify, but to complicate and confuse—perhaps as a way of protecting their profitable fiefdoms from those who do not possess their specialized knowledge. My suggestion to the Committee is that if they truly wish to legitimize and ennoble the study of economics, they need to reward research and theories that are understandable and also valuable to the society as a whole.

Dear Nobel Prize for Economics Committee,
Let me begin by commending you for encouraging insightful thinking and writing in the field of economics. The lives of everyday people are greatly affected by both politics and the

economy; but the more dominant influence is that which you survey—economics. To a certain extent politics can be ignored or avoided, but economics is all-pervasive in our daily lives. So it should be unceasingly examined and analyzed.

My purpose in writing to you is to suggest that perhaps the committee's perspective has become too narrow. The broad river of any discipline tends to branch off into tiny meandering tributaries of specialization. This creates battalions of experts who cannot see the forest because they are looking at one leaf on a single tree.

Perhaps this is an appropriate time for you to seek out and encourage economists who are generalists and not specialists. Here are some bullet point observations about the impact of economics on our planet and its creatures. Most of these conclusions are obvious to the average person in the street, but somehow they are imperceptible to those in the ivory towers.

• **Capitalism Has Mutated Into Predatory Capitalism**. A system that once encouraged individual creativity and hard work is now so totally ruled by those at the top that it has become a private club for the über-elite, who maintain their status by suppressing opportunities for all others. A perfect example is the gargantuan chain stores that bulldoze their way into community after community, destroying small local businesses wherever they go. In biology they would be deemed an "invasive species," but in contemporary economics they are honored and forgiven on the grounds that they are a "good business model."

• **Too Much Of Our Commerce No Longer Involves Goods Or Services**. The so-called "financial sector" has metastasized from a tiny portion of the economy into a Godzilla-like dominator of global markets. But the "products" that they market have almost no intrinsic or tangible value. The bankers and hedge fund managers who rule these kingdoms are sleazy conjurers who merchandise worthless "financial instruments" that are so esoteric that even their creators barely understand

them. The world simply does not need "credit default swaps."
But it does need rice in the bowls of the starving millions.

• **The Three "P's" Of Economics Are Backwards.** We currently live in a Darwinian "survival of the most ruthless" economic system. Under an Ethical Economics, the three "P's" would be reversed. Profits would be subservient to People and the Planet. This would mean that workers' jobs could not be taken away from them by robots, or "off-shored" to laborers working for slave wages in Dickensian conditions somewhere in China or Bangladesh. And the wonders of our miracle planet are not simply commodities. Forests are not just "board feet" and rivers are not latent "hydro-electric power." Worshipping "profit" is worshipping Greed.

• **"Too Big To Fail" Are Four Dirty Words.** The most enormous and powerful banks are allowed to reap obscene profits when one of their endeavors succeeds, but when one of their programs fails, the taxpayer bails them out and eliminates or minimizes their losses. This situation is so perverse that it could only have been conceived by the lobbyists for the banks. But our politicians are also complicit since they pass the legislation that allows it. They do so after receiving huge "campaign contributions" which is the deceitful way of saying "bribes." And the regulatory agencies which should be overseeing such malfeasance are packed with former executives of the very banks that they supposedly monitor.

• **Unlimited Money Printing Will Lead To Unlimited Agony.** Despite the fact that every single fiat currency in history has failed miserably, the central bankers of the world are engaged in this practice once again. But this time the consequences will be far more catastrophic because our economies are so interlinked globally that a sneeze in Brazil can lead to pneumonia for the whole world. Anyone who lived through the horror of the Weimar hyper-inflation would cringe at the possibility of such a plague spreading across the entire planet.

102

• **Infinite Growth On A Finite Planet Is Not Just Ludicrous —It Is Genocidal.** In human biology unlimited growth is known as cancer, but in economics it is considered Nirvana. Petroleum is the best example of the destructive consequences of unchecked growth. The world has become utterly dependent on affordable petroleum products for transportation, agriculture, and manufacturing, and as the supply and affordability of oil reaches critical levels, the entire panorama of modern techno-industrial society will change and probably crash. And this "threshold of collapse" scenario is also playing out in many other areas such as oceanic fish stocks, drinking water, the desertification of former farmland and many other resources. Ignoring these problems does not solve them. In fact, it exacerbates them, and the consequences might not be just terrible, but genocidal.

And so, in conclusion, as you search for future laureates for the Nobel Economics Prize, perhaps there are candidates out there who are less focused on the minutiae of the subject and are instead more conversant with the bigger picture and with its consequences. If the everyday Jane and Joe in the street can perceive the aberrations and injustices of the current economic template, surely there are experts who can also do so— and who can offer meaningful and wide-ranging improvements.

Thank you for considering my suggestions,

Ray Jason

The Solace of Haiku

*I*T WAS A SUBTLE, delicate, watercolor sunset. The sky
was not ablaze with vivid reds and oranges battling for
attention, but rather a serene panorama of gentle saffron and peach. I was seated on *Aventura*'s cabin top with my
back against the mast, drinking what I call Tarzan Tea. It is the
water of a young coconut which I have just opened with my
machete. My notepad and pen are within arm's reach as I settle in for the last stage of my Immersion Time.

It begins in the late afternoon with a vigorous swim followed by a very un-vigorous float. Lying on my back, buoyant
and content in the salty Caribbean water, I am joyously mindful that I have sculpted my life to not just enjoy Nature or visit
Nature—but to Immerse myself in it. I pull myself from the sea
into my dinghy in one smooth and powerful motion. I am wet
and sleek like my dolphin neighbors, and I feel strong and lithe
and sensuous. My thoughts turn to the hundreds of millions of
civilized humans who are incarcerated in office cubicles at
that moment, and who never—or only rarely, on a vacation—
get to experience such primal pleasure.

Back on board *Aventura*, I reposition my plastic solar
shower, which has been lying on the deck heating the sky water which flowed from my awning to my tank during last

night's squall. My refreshing hot shower uses less than two gallons of water, and while toweling myself dry, I recall one of my favorite Mark Twain aphorisms, "We have turned a thousand useless luxuries into necessities." I chuckle at the realization that I am not just a right-brain man in a left-brain world, but I am also a solar shower guy on an iPod planet.

After slicing open the young, green coconut I surrender to high-tech temptation and use a straw to drink its delicious, nourishing water. Placing the nut in a small dog bowl so that it doesn't roll over, I grab my notepad and pen. My hands are almost shaking with anticipation, because it is now the final phase of my Immersion Time. It is the Haiku Hour.

My appreciation for this simple and elegant form of Japanese poetry began in an unusual manner. The military draft had ensnared me just after college, and I was about to ship out for Vietnam on a U.S. Navy ammunition ship. On my last liberty in San Francisco before our departure, I was searching through the almost magical shelves of Lawrence Ferlinghetti's City Lights bookstore. My quest was for a book that was both enticing and small—because our shipboard lockers could barely hold our clothes and toiletries.

Suddenly a mere sliver of a book caught my attention. It was entitled *Haiku Poetry* and was written by an American named James W. Hackett. What made this tiny volume extraordinary was the fact that these were not translations of works by the great Japanese masters such as Basho or Issa, but original haiku in English. I read the first few pages and each poem was simple and exquisite. Then I switched to the final pages to see whether his later efforts had dissipated into mediocrity, but these were as perceptive and moving as the first ones.

Also in the back of the book I encountered a brief set of guidelines that he had composed to assist others who might wish to try this form. It was called "Suggestions For Writing Haiku Poetry In English." This was amazing—an author who was so in love with his art form that he wanted to selflessly share his knowledge of it with others.

At the cash register, the clerk complimented me on my selection and mentioned that there were three other books in this series. She then led me to them and I jubilantly left the great little bookshop with all four tiny volumes that weighed less than my wallet and would fit just as comfortably into a back pocket.

During those extremely difficult times aboard that ship in the Vietnam theatre, those minuscule books brought me great and abiding solace when little else was providing me any consolation. During that grim period I repeatedly attempted to compose haiku of my own, but was never satisfied with my efforts. The environment was just too antithetical to "haiku mind."

But decades later when I embraced the sea gypsy life and cocooned myself in Nature, the little poems just flowed as effortlessly as a full-moon tide. When my immersion in the Wild finally awakened my haiku sensibility, I re-visited the American master's "Suggestions" and found that their guidance remained wise and helpful. Here are the principles of his teaching that have proven most valuable in creating my poems.

Greater nature and not human nature is the place of haiku—and Now is the time of haiku. Solitude and silence are vital for interpenetrating and empathizing with the wild. Modifying words should never be superfluous, and should suggest season or location or time of day. Use verbs in the present tense and singular subjects whenever possible. Haiku should be intuitive and direct and not abstract, symbolic or intellectual. And finally, one of his suggestions is phrased so perfectly that I offer it verbatim: "Remember that haiku is a finger pointing at the moon, and if the hand is bejeweled, we no longer see that to which it points."

It is now over forty years since those tiny books inspired and comforted me. I think of them every night at dusk when I sit on my little boat nestled between the sea and the sky with my notepad and my pen and my fervent desire to once again discover my "haiku mind." Here are some of my poems. I call them Sea Gypsy Haiku and I hope that they bring you a smile— or a surprise—or some solace of your own.

The sea gypsy life—
all of my neighbors live in
the sea and the sky.

A mother dolphin
shows her baby—clouds of fish—
and seas of wonder.

You noisy parrots—
always chirping when you fly.
Do you sing of Joy?

No road before me—
vanishing wake behind me—
sea gypsy freedom!

Four egrets flying
so close that they look like a
single eight-winged bird.

Happy fisherman—
a little rum, a full moon,
and perhaps a fish.

Safely at anchor—
a night breeze cools the cabin—
sea gypsy heaven!

Not just a great blue—
your enormous wings make you
a huge blue heron!

Weary sea gypsy—
a kindly woman shares her
house of happiness.

Twin brothers rowing
their cayuco perfectly.
Oarsmen in the womb?

A white sail passing
on the distant horizon—
deep sea loneliness.

Native fisherman
laughs at the rain—if the fish
don't mind, why should he?

Ocean reverie—
wind and wave and sky and stars.
What more is needed?

Moon path on the sea
tempts my sailboat to seek
the endless horizon.

Bright stars in the sky,
luminescence in the sea—
ocean harmony!

Terror is Never Sacred

A HANDSOME CATAMARAN recently docked near my lovely sailboat. The captain is Russian and his wife is Turkish. They have two children, and although they are too young to sign their own passports, I suspect that they are from the Kingdom of Joy. That's because all day long they spread their laughter and happiness throughout the marina. Whether it is riding their tiny bicycles or fishing with their parents or trying to learn how to swim, their vibrant innocence delights and comforts me.

It has also inspired me. The essay that I had been working on seemed lost in a mental labyrinth. It deals with the immense subject of religion, and it had become too big and too confused. But then a wave and a smile from the two kids suddenly made me realize that I should narrow my focus, and concentrate on religion and children.

* * *

The Ultimate Terror

Witnessing the carefree exuberance of these youngsters brings me both joy and sorrow. I am happy that they live so effortlessly in the ecstasy of the moment, and that their youth shields them from the woes of the world. But I am sad that all around the world hundreds of millions of children are having such blissful contentment sacrificed on the altar of hell.

How do we not understand that churches that preach hellfire are the most evil terrorist organizations on the planet? The worst that a political enemy can do is torture and murder a person. At least that victim's suffering ends with their death. But if a Christian fails to abide by certain rules, they are supposedly doomed to eternal fire and damnation. And if a person i s not a Christian, they too are sentenced to endless fiery agony.

If such a virulent dogma was imposed on people when they arrived at adulthood, at least they would have enough life experience to evaluate it. But forcing such a terrifying vision on an unknowing child is so repellent that I can't find a word for it. Oh wait, here's a good one—despicable.

Consider, for a moment, the child-raising process. Human nurturing revolves around the parents steadily and incrementally passing along life lessons to their offspring. The kids learn that snakes can be deadly, that deep water can drown them, and that fire can kill them. As this knowledge is passed along to the children, a bond of trust is established. So when the parents claim that there is this horrible place called hell, where bad people suffer eternal torture, the child believes that as well.

And so their world, which had been a magical, immediate, constantly-unfolding realm of wonder, is suddenly darkened and poisoned by the horror of hell. Destroying the innocence, optimism and joy of youth with such a doctrine is an indisputable act of terror!

But even more appalling is the fact that it is also an act of deceit: there is utterly no way that a parent or a priest or even a pope can absolutely know that there is a hell, and yet they proclaim that this is the case. When someone insists that something is true even though they cannot prove it, that per-son is telling a lie.

And how do the hellfire-spreaders defend such a perverse dogma? They insist that without the threat of eternal incinera-tion, these children would not behave themselves. And yet the huge portion of the world that is not hypnotized by hellfire re-ligions (such as the Hindus, Buddhists, and non-believers gen-erally) do not rampage around the planet wreaking havoc upon it. Even though nobody is screaming at them from a pul-pit with threats of devils and pitchforks, these people manage to behave with decency and compassion.

So this is my first example of how religion is profoundly harmful to children—it mutilates the innocence and wonder of youth with the terror of a hell whose existence cannot be proven.

Morality Does Not Need Religion

One of the common defenses of religion is that it is the key-stone that keeps the arch of morality from collapsing in ruin. This is a preposterous claim that is easy to disprove. There were about 10,000 generations of humanity that preceded the appearance of the sky-god monotheisms that dominate today's religious landscape—or should that be battlefield? Without any commandments from Hebraic gods, these people managed to discover enough moral principles to not destroy each other and thus they carried on the human line.

Furthermore, throughout history there have been hundreds of other religions that arose, prospered, declined and disap-peared. As each of these disintegrated, there was no wide-spread chaos and carnage even though their ethical precepts had vanished.

Moral knowledge—the awareness of the difference between right and wrong—is innate in all of us. We do not need priests or mullahs or rabbis to reveal it to us. The revered ten commandments are a perfect example of this: Four of them are just a megalomaniacal insistence on reverence toward one particular god, and the other six are essentially self-evident. Any New Guinea hunter-gatherer has figured out these things without the need for stone tablets.

Rather than being essential to morality, I find that religion is actually a keystone of *immorality*. For decades I have been arguing that the most far-reaching way to improve the world is to replace religion with Basic Human Decency. Consider this short list of things that you cannot do in the name of basic human decency, but that you can do in the name of Jesus or Mohammed:

- Witch hunts
- Suicide bombings
- Inquisitions
- Book burnings
- Holy wars
- Female oppression
- Slavery
- Homosexual bigotry
- Ethnic cleansing
- Unwanted children
- Demonization of scientists

One of the main reasons that religion is such a malignant rather than benign force is because it immediately allied itself with the kings and pharaohs after the arrival of so-called human civilization. Before agriculture, in the long Paleolithic hunter-gatherer era, there was no hierarchal division of rulers and ruled. But when Neolithic agriculture provided food surpluses and then division of labor, this also initiated what I call "division of importance." In simple terms, this means a society comprised of a tiny elite of dominant people and a huge mass of subordinate people.

Those that ascended to the top of the political class tended to be the most ruthless and immoral. And since religious leaders wanted to be the handmaidens of these pitiless demagogues, they camouflaged their immoral deeds with moral platitudes. They had already sold their souls even as they were claiming that their mission was to save them.

* * *

As I sit with my back against the mast, finishing this essay, the two beautiful children come scurrying past. A few steps behind them are their parents, carrying tiny swimming goggles and life jackets. As they disappear down the dock this little scene of happiness somehow inverts itself in my mind's eye. And I realize that halfway around the world there are two other parents sobbing in almost unbearable agony as they hold their dead child in their arms. Ten minutes earlier she had been the joy and blessing of their lives—a bundle of sunshine in human form.

I wonder on which of the current killing fields of the Holy Land this sad event is unfolding. Is it Gaza, where one religion opposes another? Or is it Iraq where the carnage is even more perverse—since it is between warring sects of the same religion?

I quietly curse all of the senseless, cruel tragedy of life as I sit here pondering it from the evening of my years. And then I wonder about the future of those precious children on the nearby boat, who are only in the daybreak of their years. Will their twilight decades see a planet that has been purged of this evil force? Will their children get to savor a new golden dawn emancipated from this curse which has caused so much horror and suffering down the centuries?

I will not pray for this... but I will yearn for it... and I will work for it!

115

Rhapsody on a Theme by Socrates

*H*OW COULD I *not* love a place called Gypsy Island? Isla Gitana is how you say it in Spanish, but a few years before my arrival, it had a slightly less romantic name, Isla Muertos—Island of the Dead. That's because part of it was a burial ground. The locals had deliberately located it on an island far enough out in the Gulf of Nicoya so that the ghosts could not swim to the mainland. In fact, in the months that I was there, they weren't even able to make it out to *Aventura*—even though she was anchored only 30 yards from the shore.

My sojourn at Isla Gitana was both tranquil and rambunctious, with great new friendships and rollicking adventures. But the highlight was surely the day that an actual Tall Ship anchored beside *Aventura*. She was the *Pacific Swift* out of Vancouver—a sail training vessel full of bright, inquisitive teenagers out to see the world and gather some life lessons.

When the kids would go ashore they would pile into their two longboats and row gracefully and powerfully to a nearby dock. On Christmas Eve there were about 10 boats in the anchorage, and when nightfall descended, the longboats visited every one of the yachts. Each of the teens had a songbook and a long, thin candle with a little collar to protect their hands

117

from the dripping wax. They serenaded each sailboat crew with a lovely, heartfelt Christmas carol. When they arrived at *Aventura* they chose "O Holy Night." As they drifted away to go sing for the next boat, I realized how truly "holy" that night was. What could be more sacred than this little unspoiled bay —which was my idea of a real cathedral—made even more sublime by this touching display of human affection?

A few days later as they sailed away, I blew my conch shell in salute, and the kids all waved and smiled enthusiastically. I had grown so fond of them in their time there that as their ship rounded the headland on her way back out into the Pacific, an unusual idea occurred to me. What if their onboard teacher had gotten sick, and the Captain had asked me to substitute as their instructor for a few days? The skipper and I had shared a few beers ashore during their visit, and he had been intrigued by my contrary-to-ordinary philosophical approach to life. And what if he had encouraged me to "not hold back" when it came to sharing my unconventional worldview? And so to fend off the melancholy of the *Pacific Swift's* departure, I spent most of that day pondering what my first lecture to the young student/sailors might have included. It went something like this:

Good morning, everyone. Most of you already know me, but for those of you who don't, my name is Ray. Your Captain has gifted me with this extraordinary opportunity to be your guest instructor for a few days while your regular teacher recovers from his illness. I am particularly delighted by your skipper's trust in me, because I am not a credentialed teacher—I am a thoughtful wanderer.

I am going to begin by playing three minutes of classical music for you. It is a movement from Rachmaninoff's famous piano concerto called "Rhapsody on a Theme by Paganini." Now that you have heard it, let me explain why I started with it. My belief is that the purpose of human life is to not just *exist* but to *flourish*. And I believe that the haunting crescendos of that music are a sublime example of how the human spirit can in fact *soar*—and that our species is indeed capable of majesty and beauty.

Just as Rachmaninoff elaborated on some themes of the great violinist Paganini, I wish to discuss some themes inspired by one of history's virtuoso philosophers—Socrates. In particular, for our lesson today I have chosen this enduring aphorism from the Greek master: "The unexamined Life is not worth living." And so the title for this introductory lecture is "Rhapsody on a theme by Socrates."

First of all, I recognize that as student/sailors aboard a "semester-at-sea" tall ship, you are receiving a far more unconventional education than those back in the normal school systems, and I applaud your program in this regard. However, my desire during my few days as your substitute instructor is to deeply challenge what I suspect may be some of your most cherished beliefs. The reason that I wish to do so is because education has detoured from its core mission—which is to train people in how to be critical thinkers.

Teachers have become too complacent when it comes to challenging society's accepted wisdom. Largely, this is because genuinely radical instructors who inspire their students to carefully examine a culture's myths and values are a severe threat to the powers that benefit from the status quo. Therefore, such mentors are often ostracized. This leads to a world full of timid teachers who do not exalt you to consider life deeply as Socrates urged his students to do.

For example, how often has a teacher presented you with an alternative interpretation of the Christopher Columbus mythology? Since we are all here on a magnificent sailing ship, this is an excellent starting point for my attempt to stimulate your critical thinking.

Columbus is an exceedingly important historical figure. Here are two pieces of evidence to prove this assertion. He is one of only four individuals to have a national holiday in the

U.S. He joins Washington, Lincoln and Martin Luther King in this elite category. And secondly, he is so pivotal that historical timelines are designated as "Pre- or Post-Columbian."

His actions were so significant that they essentially carved the template for over 500 years of white, male dominator behavior in the Americas. In my estimation he is one of the most whitewashed figures in human history. My schoolbooks depicted him as Columbus the Hero; but the indigenous people of any of the lands that he visited—and, hopefully, some of your teachers and books—portray him very differently. In fact, they might be challenged by picking which despicable description to apply to him. Should they choose Columbus the Ruthless or the Obscene or the Vicious or the Hideous or the Vile or... all of the above?

Here is my assessment of Christopher Columbus: he was a genocidal megalomaniac. The sources of my evidence are as good as they get—primary journal entries from Columbus himself and from some of the crewmen and priests who sailed with him.

Here is the man's legacy: he bequeathed the New World two of the worst institutions in human history—the Slave and the Conquistador. It would take about 350 years for people of conscience to finally rid the world of slavery. And the Conquistador evil is still widespread on our planet. At this very moment there are indigenous tribes in the Amazon trying to protect their land and their way of life from lumber and cattle barons. And in Ecuador, international oil companies are destroying the habitat of jungle tribes whose ancestors lived there long before the word "petroleum" was even invented.

Genocide is the murder of a large number of people of one racial or ethnic strain. But Columbus did not just kill an enormous number—he actually eradicated the Taino Indians from the face of the earth. When he first landed in Hispaniola (currently shared by Haiti and the Dominican Republic) it was estimated that there were around 1.2 million natives there. By

1550—less than 60 years later—there was not a single one left. And from almost the moment that his ships arrived, these gentle Indians suffered an almost incomprehensible reign of terror.

The vicious power that Columbus and his sailors possessed was not the result of superior strength or intelligence or courage. It rested solely on having more advanced technology in the form of ocean-going ships and deadly weapons. To demonstrate his ruthless omnipotence, Columbus would punish Indians in the most hideous manner for minor offenses. He would command that a nose or an ear be chopped off as a reminder to the rest of the population that he ruled supreme.

His merciless actions became so insufferable that mass suicides, where 100 people would jump from a cliff, became commonplace. Women stopped trying to have children and would strangle their newborns rather than allow them to live and endure the agonies of the Spaniards. And along with the normal slavery of converting people into beasts of burden, Columbus also initiated sex slavery. He even bragged in letters back to the Old World that the most favored girls were only 9 or 10 years old. So, one can add pedophilia to his crimes against humanity.

As for his megalomania, what title did he insist on receiving from his royal patrons as payment for the slaves and stolen property that he brought back to Spain? His humble request was to be called "Admiral of the Ocean Seas." Since this essentially includes all of the world's oceans, it was comparable to a land-based dictator wishing to be addressed as the "Emperor of Earth."

But beyond his atrocities and his arrogance, this is why I despise Columbus: as long as we honor him rather than scorn him, we are reinforcing his code of conduct. In its most basic rendering, it is that domination trumps decency. His modus operandi was to exercise raw power whenever it suited his desires. If a native population had something that he wanted and they would not surrender it, then he would take it from them by force.

This same immoral approach to human affairs dominates our planet to this day. It is somewhat more subtle, but nonetheless it is still basically the strong imposing their will on the weak. We camouflage it better today with words like democracy or capitalism or free trade or globalization but at its core it is the "haves" ruling the "have-nots."

But enough of me ranting here on the foredeck of our beautiful floating classroom—it is time for some of your input. Please raise your hand if you have a question or a comment. Wow! now there is an enthusiastic response that would have delighted Socrates himself. I'll happily take all of your questions one by one. But first let me share a little anecdote with you that clarifies my philosophy about the student/teacher relationship.

A few decades ago there was a wonderful movie house in San Francisco called the Surf Theater. As the name suggests, it was located out by the ocean. It specialized in classic and foreign and unusual films. Back in those pre-multiplex days, it was common to post three separate prices. Typically for seniors and students it might be $3 and the regular price would be $5. But the Surf charged the same $4 for everybody. This nonconformist approach was explained by a simple sign placed in the window of the ticket booth. It amuses and inspires me as much today as it did the very first time that I saw it. That little sign packed a lot of wisdom into four words. It said: "We Are All Students!"

The Sea Gypsy Tribe Start-Up Manual

*E*ARLIER IN THIS BOOK, I proposed an unusual response to the possibility of global societal collapse that previously has not been suggested. My core message was summed up in these 30 words:

"I believe that if there is a near-extinction catastrophe, a sea gypsy tribe has the best chance of both surviving and replenishing the human population in the wisest manner."

That piece provides the "why-to" background information for my belief that economic, energy and ecological disasters are very possible in our near future. It then suggests that various sea gypsy tribes scattered about the planet provide an excellent survival and re-seeding option. *This* article provides the basic "how-to" information for anyone who was inspired by my message and would like to join our movement. My sense is that there are three potential types of candidates. I refer to them as Seekers, Converts and Recruits.

The Seekers are skilled ocean sailors who are already out there cruising, but who are searching for more meaning in their vagabond lives. The frenzied, hollow, shop-till-you-drop, electronic do-dad hologram that modern life has become was no longer tolerable, so they sought the comfort and authenticity of Mother Ocean. Hopefully, my essay awoke them to the probability that there are many other liked-minded sailors out there who are also looking for their tribe.

The second category is the Converts. This group is also already out there enjoying the cruising life in their ocean-ready sailboats. But their basic philosophy is very different from that of the Seekers. Here is a good way to describe the conversion that would be necessary for them to be drawn towards the sea gypsy tribal value system: If they previously thought that the American Dream was good for the planet, but now realize that it is extremely destructive of the planet, then they are ready to hoist their Earth Flags and join our clan.

I classify the third group as Recruits. They have no sailing experience, but they are mindful of the lunacy of modern life and are searching for other, more fulfilling paths. Many of the core sea gypsy tribal values resonate with them. They understand that infinite growth on a finite planet is delusional. They sense that the vast problems caused by too much technology cannot be fixed with more technology. And they do not want to contribute their energy and vision to an increasingly more Orwellian police/surveillance State. They are fed up, and they wish they had a boat and knew how to sail it.

The main purpose of this essay is to convince those Recruits that they *can* learn how to sail and they *should* buy a boat. Also, I wish to reassure them that this can be done much more quickly and affordably than they might imagine. As for the Seekers and Converts, my purpose is to help them upgrade their cruising sailboats into state-of-the-art, ocean-going survival pods. Let's begin!

* * *

Learning To Sail. The vast majority of sailors are *not* wealthy yachtsmen. They are regular people who learned their skills without spending a fortune doing so. Your local Parks and Recreation Department will often have low-cost sailing instruction. Don't be put off if it looks like the lessons will be conducted in tiny boats—it's actually best to learn in small craft because they are so responsive to the moodiness of the wind.

There are also low-cost sailing clubs in many towns as well as programs offered through community colleges; the backs of most sailing magazines will also list programs where you can learn sailing. The costs range from reasonable to extravagant, but if you're looking to go no-cost, try hitting the docks at your local marina. Most sailors are pleasant, easygoing people, and if you express an interest in learning and offer to swap some help with boat projects, you have a good chance of picking up some instruction in return.

Volunteering to crew on local racing boats is another option. You will initially be given simple tasks, but if you pay attention, you can swiftly learn a lot. There are many "how-to" books that provide excellent instruction on the basics of sailing. Many libraries will carry some of these. Otherwise, they can easily be Googled up.

So, as you can see from the preceding inventory, there are lots of ways to learn basic sailing. Once that is achieved you will need to acquire "cruising skills." In a way this is even easier, because the sailing magazines run a steady stream of articles dealing with topics such as anchoring, dinghy selection, outboard motor repair, food provisioning, navigation, and various potential emergencies at sea. A couple of inexpensive subscriptions to sailing magazines would provide you lots of valuable information, and many libraries have current and back issues of these periodicals. Another excellent, inexpensive resource is the U.S. Coast Guard Auxiliary. They offer many free and low-cost courses in such topics as safe boat handling, first-aid and coastal navigation.

* * *

Buying A Sailboat. Just as there are many options for learning how to sail, there are also lots of ways to find a suitable boat that can be both your joy and your protector. When friends ask for suggestions, I recommend fiberglass boats in the 30- to 45-foot range. My preference for fiberglass is because they are light but strong. They are also low-maintenance, and since they are the most prevalent on the market, they tend to be reasonably priced. There are certainly merits to the other hull materials—steel, aluminum, wood and ferro-cement—so if that is your preference, indulge it!

My size recommendation is based on the fact that the majority of the sea gypsy community is likely to be couples. Less than 30 feet and things get a bit cramped; more than 45 feet and the vessel becomes difficult for just 2 people to handle. Additionally, the 45-foot size should adequately take care of the needs of families with kids.

While you are learning basic sailing, you will probably start noticing boats that appeal to you. Owners love it when a stranger approaches them and says, "That sure is a fine looking boat... what kind is she?" By window-shopping your nearby docks and by paying attention to the boats in the magazines you can become fairly knowledgeable quite swiftly.

Here is another important tip for quickly increasing your knowledge: Go to a website called yachtworld.com, then click on their "brokerage" section and type in specifics such as "used, sail, fiberglass, 35 to 45 feet and under $60k." Most of the listings that pop up will have multiple photos of the exteriors and the interiors as well as the "specs" for each vessel.

Once you have a better sense of your needs and wishes, you can get serious in your search. Start locally by walking the nearby docks and searching for boats with "for sale" signs. Check the classifieds in your local newspaper and also in any free "shopper" papers. There are also regional editions of *Sailboat Trader* which can usually be found at convenience stores.

Many sailboat designs have "owners' groups" who find each other on the Web and exchange information about their boats. So, for example, if you found yourself desiring the venerable old Pearson 424 design, you could Google up their owners' page and see if they know of any sister ships for sale.

There are many listings in the back of the sailing magazines. Besides the glossy national publications, there are several regional ones that are published on newsprint that are also very helpful. *Latitude 38*, which originates from San Francisco, is a good example; almost all are free, and almost all have complimentary online versions.

And, of course, there are also professional boat brokers. These folks are quite different from the typical used car salesman who is trying to close the deal while you are there on the lot. Brokers realize the magnitude of your purchase, and they don't try to rush you into a decision. Most marinas will have some brokerages nearby, or you can locate them in the yellow pages or online. And speaking of the differences between buying a car and a sailboat, you'll be happy to learn about professional yacht surveyors. These are specialists who carefully examine vessels and then make a thorough written report of their strengths and deficiencies. For "cash and a handshake" purchases this is not necessary; however, banks and insurance companies require this, and considering the value of the investment, a survey is usually well worth the expense.

* * *

Outfitting Your Boat. Hopefully, my suggestions will help you find your dream boat. When that happy day arrives, your focus will then shift to preparing her for the rigors and joys of the open ocean. There are a few excellent books to help guide you through this process. My favorite is *Ready For Sea* by Tor Pinney, because it is well written and contains a wealth of information that is understandable even to a novice.

It is important to emphasize that ocean sailboats are complex creatures. There are *many* systems that are vital to a boat that are not needed in your house, apartment, condo, or yurt. Here is a list of some of them:

Anchors, autopilots, bilge pumps, diesels, dinghies, GPS, ham and SSB radios, life-rafts, outboard motors, radars, roller-furlers, solar panels, winches, wind generators, windlasses.

This might seem daunting, but most used boats on the market are already equipped with many of these systems. And more importantly, that less-complicated but stationary house will not help you escape in the case of a societal meltdown. I could devote thousands of words to arguing the merits of any of these pieces of gear, but it is far better for the novice to research this on their own. Pore through the magazines and "how-to" books and ask other sailors on your docks. Another excellent source for information on properly outfitting your boat is the West Marine catalog, which the company makes available free of charge. Scattered within its pages are short "advisors" on just about every system and piece of hardware you'll ever need.

* * *

Specific Sea Gypsy Tribe Preparations. Everything that I have described thus far would apply to anyone who wanted to wander the wide waters on their own sailboat. Now, I will outline some specific preparations for long-term self-reliance in case civilized society starts to unravel. I emphasize that my hope is that this will never occur, nor am I claiming that it will occur. But there is much wisdom in "hoping for the best, but preparing for the worst!" This is the portion of this essay that is directed not just to the "Recruits" but also to the "Converts" and the "Seekers."

The most vital needs in a survival situation are probably:

Water Food Shelter Protection
Communications

Water. A human can survive for weeks without food, but only for a few days without water. On a sailboat there are two basic ways to stay supplied with drinking water. The low-cost option is to "catch" water directly from rain showers. I call this "sky water," and it is delicious. I use an awning that dips towards its mid-point and funnels the rain through a hose directly into my tanks. I let the first couple of minutes of rain wash the awning clean, hook the hose up to the tanks, and then a foot-pump down at the galley sends the water to a Brita pitcher. In my decades of cruising I have never run out of water, and that includes ocean passages of up to 30 days.

The second option is a reverse-osmosis water-maker that converts sea water into fresh water. There are both manual and electric versions. The electric ones are low-maintenance and only need to be run for a short period each day; some of them can also be pumped manually if there is a problem with your ship's electrical supply. As for the problem of oceanic acidification, none of my friends with water-makers say that this has become an issue, and I assume that the manufacturers are paying close attention to this and beefing up their systems.

Food. Non-perishable foods are the mainstay of a survival vessel. Most sailboats have refrigeration systems that can be powered by solar panels and/or wind generators. But these fridges are mostly devoted to lengthening the edibility of perishable foods such as meat, dairy products and vegetables. On an extended voyage, or if supplies ashore are cut off, the fridge will just become a glorified beer cooler.

Nowadays, many more boats are using freezers, which greatly increase the length of time one can keep perishable food on board. However, these use far more energy, usually requiring the diesel or generator to be run for an hour or more each day. As this essay foresees a world without readily available petroleum, a freezer may not be a truly practical option for a survival vessel.

Because I have always been on the impoverished end of the sea gypsy financial spectrum, I have mostly sailed without refrigeration. But I have not suffered because of this. A quick inspection of my ship's cupboards reveals the following wealth of long-term foods that are readily available from any grocery store:

Almonds, beef stew, black beans, Bragg's liquid aminos, brown rice, canned beef, canned chicken, canned clams, canned fruits, canned salmon, canned shrimp, canned soups, canned veggies, cashews, cereal, crackers, dried fruits, egg noodles, fruit cocktail, garbanzo beans, Gouda cheese, honey, jelly, lentils, long-life bread, long-life milk , macaroni and cheese, mayo, nutritional yeast, oatmeal, paella mix, pancake mix, pasta, peanut butter, powdered, eggs, powdered milk, protein powder, red beans, salami, sardines, spaghetti, sugar, tea, tofu, TSP (Textured Soy Protein), whole wheat flour, etc.

This inventory should demonstrate that eating aboard an ocean-capable sailboat is not just beans-and rice drudgery. Furthermore, I supplement these supplies with freeze-dried and dehydrated foods. I have dozens of large #10 cans filled with such treats as beef stroganoff, chicken teriyaki and dehydrated broccoli. A little water and a very short cooking time and you have delicious meals.

I also keep a supply of canned bacon, cheese and butter aboard. If you Google up "survival foods" you will find many sources for purchasing these extremely valuable products. Growing my own alfalfa and mung bean sprouts has been a tradition aboard *Aventura* for many years. A large jar of these tiny seeds will provide you months of tasty sprouts that are alive with nutrition.

There are also old sailors' tricks for extending the life of perishable foods without refrigeration. For example, potatoes, carrots, onions and cabbage will last quite some time if stored in cool, dark locations. Raw eggs can be coated in Vaseline to extend their usability, and I wrap apples, oranges and zucchinis in aluminum foil to help keep them fresh.

An important component of the onboard, long-term food supply will be fishing and foraging. Fish, lobster and crab from the sea and clams, mussels, and oysters from the shore are all mighty fine and nutritious foods. Seaweed is also something that will prove very valuable, although I personally need to learn much more about identifying and harvesting the best types.

Food drying, especially of fruit, seaweed and fish, is also an area that requires more of my attention. I look forward to increasing my knowledge and therefore my food independence as I research this. Thus far my web surfing has failed to locate a good, affordable solar food dryer; while there are plenty of electric ones available, they must run for hours and as such are a huge drain on the ship's electrical supply. However, there are nice solar ovens and cookers already available, and one of them is high on my wish list. Sun-baked bread is reportedly quite delicious.

In concluding this vital section, it should be emphasized that a well-provisioned sailboat can be an island of comfort and safety as the food procuring situation dangerously deteriorates for those stranded on the land during any severe catastrophe.

Shelter. A person in his or her sailboat is like a turtle in its shell—you bring your own house with you. This also allows you to bring along a nice supply of creature comforts as well. My library is a constant joy for me, and positioned beside it is a nice selection of movies on DVD which I can watch on this very laptop. Plus I have plenty of music CDs onboard as well.

High-end boats with water-makers and propane water heaters provide hot showers even a thousand miles from land. And if there is no longer any propane, they can shower as I have contentedly done for years, by using a very low-priced but effective solar shower.

Being able to move your comfortable shelter is probably its greatest feature. If I was in the U.S. and some sort of societal meltdown began, I could depart in a matter of hours. I keep my diesel fuel, water tanks, propane supply and food always topped off. I would bid farewell to my local friends, email my more distant ones, go buy fresh fruit and meats and veggies, check the weather forecast online and get under way.

I would then set a course for one of my favorite non-First-World countries—probably in Central America. There are well-considered reasons for this choice. Because their basic infra - structure is *less* reliable than ours, they have adjusted to disruptions and can handle them better. Having experienced previous problems with the transportation of food, they usually have a supply stock-piled and won't become violently upset by the trucks not arriving. And, they don't have the "entitlement" issues of the citizens of the wealthier countries that make them so dependent on governmental assistance. Essentially, these folks have always demonstrated a better capacity to fend for themselves.

Protection. In my Sea Gypsy Tribe essay I emphasized the tremendous danger that starving, heavily-armed marauders pose to land-based people. My belief is that the only real strategy for avoiding this life-threatening likelihood is to *leave*. In my carefully considered opinion, staying onshore and attempting to win a seemingly endless series of firefights to protect one's family and food is a fool's mission.

But what about the hazards that might exist "out there?" Let's begin by talking about piracy. Most of the attacks that draw a lot of media attention are directed towards large ships, not at small sailboats. When there are incidents involving cruisers, the word gets out so quickly through ham and single-sideband radio nets that it is easy to avoid the problem areas. Essentially, there are only a few dangerous regions and since we know where they are, we don't sail there. Would you vacation in Afghanistan?

Many, if not most, countries force you to surrender any guns that you have onboard when you clear in with Customs and Immigration. Failure to do so can result in fines, jail time and confiscation of your boat. But the likelihood of any sort of attack is greater when close to shore than it is in open waters. So, just when you might need your weapon, it is locked up in the customs office. Some sailors deal with this dilemma by hiding things deep in the boat during the inspection process, and then moving them to a more readily-accessible spot when the authorities leave.

There are legal forms of protection with less stopping power but still considerable impact, such as flare guns, pepper spray, crossbows and spear guns. There are also adaptor kits available that allow a flare gun to fire a shotgun shell rather than a flare.

One of the hallmarks of my personal defense strategy is that I would *never* use lethal force just to stop a thief. If someone is threatening me or a loved one with bodily injury, I would definitely respond appropriately, but I would not shoot my spear gun into the back of someone trying to steal my dinghy.

If I felt someone hop aboard my boat, I would keep my hatches shut and blast them with my air horn from down below while switching my deck lights on and off. If that did not convince them to leave, I would proceed to more assertive tactics. One protective layer that I still need to investigate is a simple car alarm-style horn that I could activate from down below if I sensed an intruder. The motion-activated ones are not ideal onboard because boats are often moving due to waves and wakes. But a manual one might be a very effective deterrent.

Communications. Often when there is a severe natural disaster such as an earthquake, the normal communication systems are completely disabled. The same would be the case in a "grid-down" emergency. In such situations the first on the scene reports are usually transmitted via ham radio operators. The reason for this is because there is no intermediary infrastructure involved, no cell phone towers or underground cables or bundles of fiber optic strands. As long as the receiving and transmitting radios are functioning, communication is possible. And since these radios can easily remain charged up using solar panels and wind generators, the ocean sailor has a far more reliable communication system than people back onshore. In a potential collapse situation this is not just comforting but potentially lifesaving.

* * *

Conclusion. In my Sea Gypsy Tribe essay I have attempted to convince whoever is willing to listen that brutally hard times might await humanity, and that the best way to survive such catastrophes is by escaping on a well-equipped ocean-ready sailboat. But besides just evading these disasters, the various sea gypsy tribes scattered upon the wide waters can also help repopulate the planet. Hopefully as they do so, they can avoid the horrible mistakes that techno-industrial civilization made. My dream is that they will create a Humanity 3.0 that will bequeath us Mozart without the mushroom cloud.

Sailing Away from Insaneistan

*M*Y NEW NEIGHBORS seem to like me. This is quite lovely—because they are dolphins. And it is even more wondrous because they are a mother and her child. Today is the fourth morning in a row that they swam a lazy circle around my boat.

Each day I greet the sunrise with an enthusiastic blast from my conch shell. It connects me with my post-civilized, feral self. It also seems to amuse the nearby creatures of the sea and the sky. No people are disturbed, because I am the only human animal in the vicinity. More importantly, it attracts the mom and her baby dolphin. They arrive just after I serenade the sun with my tribal horn.

Yesterday, the little Indio boy who sells me fresh coconuts from his tiny cayuco also brought along a live chicken. Although he offered her at a good price, I declined. But I did buy some of her eggs. Their yolks are so intensely orange that they match the morning sun nudging above the hazy horizon. They are tasty and nutritious and perfect with my Tarzan Tea.

I call my neighborhood the Archipelago of Bliss. It bequeaths me immense joy, mostly because it is totally removed from the "real world." As I sit here with my notepad and pen, I am completely severed from anything modern, and totally immersed in many things primal. Everything around me is ancient and elemental. This same type of flora and fauna has been here for over 100,000 years. The mangroves, the howler monkeys, the birds in the shallows—all preceded any human presence.

I call my slow, simple life the Way of RATAWI. That is an acronym I created which stands for Reading and Thinking and Writing Inspirationally. My day revolves around those axis pursuits. Interspersed with them are swimming, rowing, exploring, healthy eating and observing my neighbors—be they animals, clouds or planets.

When I need supplies or fellowship, it takes only a few hours to sail back to a little town abundant with eccentric characters —sailors, backpackers and surfers. Usually, about a week of visiting friends, replenishing my cupboards, and emailing out essays is sufficient. Then I head back out to whichever vacant anchorage suits my fancy.

* * *

Needless to say, most modern people would find this sort of existence... terrifying! The lack of around-the-clock stimulation and incessant electronic connectivity would be barely survivable. Even my friends, who seemingly find merit in my life path, are probably troubled by it on some level. "I mean, come on, Ray, this sea gypsy stuff is fine for a while, but isn't it time you came home?"

When I respond to such well-intentioned counsel by explaining that my life is blissfully happy and meaningful, they chalk it up to my lifelong, unrepentant romanticism. But it is not my romantic disposition that inspires me to surrender to the embrace of nature. On the contrary, it is my capacity for perceiving reality that keeps me out here wandering the wide waters.

My exile from the Great Frenzy grants me a much clearer perspective on it. If you stand a foot away from the Statue of Liberty you will not see it as well as you would from 100 yards away. Because they are so close to it, my friends cannot perceive how degraded the USA has become. Yet from afar, it is so obvious that I now not-so-jokingly refer to it as Insaneistan!

* * *

Although many react to this tragic decline with anger, my response is sadness. The founding documents of the United States are so brilliantly enlightened that they almost take one's breath away. As someone who is aware of more than just the whitewashed version of U.S. history, I realize that from the very beginning we did not live up to many of the principles in the Declaration of Independence or the Constitution. (Slavery and Native American genocide are the obvious examples.) But the concept of government of, by and for the People was such an improvement over rule by monarchs or mullahs that it deserves the utmost admiration.

And there were periods when America did seem to be that inspirational Beacon on the Hill. We had citizen legislators rather than professional politicians. We got things done that are of genuine value to the planet, such as the Panama Canal. And we interceded to subdue vicious tyrants, as in WWII.

But shortly after our greatest triumph, the seeds of our tragic demise were sown. When the evil of Hitler was vanquished, we did not dismantle our war machine as we had done after WWI. Instead, the Military Industrial Complex made its gruesome entrance onto the global stage. An enormous secret alliance of military and industrial and financial and espionage beasts spawned a lurid Leviathan that needs to engorge itself on Perpetual War in order to survive. President Eisenhower warned us about this monster in his farewell address, but his message went unheeded.

As a result, money and madness wormed their way into the American body politic like devouring parasites. Now we are controlled and manipulated by "career politicians." We no longer build canals; instead we sell high-tech weapons of death and mutilation. And rather than playing the role of schoolyard monitor to the world, we have become its most feared and hated bully.

This is not just personal opinion; this is verifiable fact. Most of the members of Congress are not schoolteachers or shop owners. They are multimillionaires who enrich themselves even further once they are in office. In a Republic, elected officials are supposed to represent the needs and interests of the people. Here is a short list of things that our government has imposed upon us in recent decades. I bet that neither you, nor anyone you know, asked for any of these.

• More than a dozen separate spy agencies which can't seem to communicate with each other, yet have no problem invading every aspect of anybody's personal life—including phone calls, emails, online purchases, etc.

• Economic and monetary policies that enrich Wall Street and the obscenely wealthy, while destroying Main Street and the middle class.

• The militarization of local police forces. With tanks and battlefield equipment, they look like Galactic Stormtroopers rather than friendly neighborhood cops. Is the police mandate still to protect the citizens and solve crimes, or are they "gearing up" for expected mass social uprisings?

• An Imperial foreign policy with over 700 military bases in more than 110 countries blanketing the planet. Our "statesmen" claim that this global presence is in our national interest and enhances our safety. But only a fool fails to see that this overreach is spawning new terrorists every day, which actually *decreases* our security.

• The perpetual misallocation of money and mind-power on the development of ever more horrific weapons of needless destruction. The litany seems endless, because it *is* endless! Atomic bombs, hydrogen bombs, neutron bombs, napalm, Agent Orange, chemical weapons, depleted uranium, white phosphorus, biological weapons and drones. And now the DARPA maniacs are working on robot soldiers, weapons in space, and cyber combat.

• The privatization of prisons. By making incarceration a "growth industry" they have incentivized the imprisonment of our sons, daughters and neighbors. And what kind of heinous criminals are we being protected from? Mostly drug users and minor dealers. The prison industrial complex is a shameful, hideous racket.

Now that I have shared this little "government in action" sampler with you, I'll repeat my question from a few paragraphs ago: "Did you, or anyone you know, ask for any of these things?"

* * *

Unfortunately it is not just politics that has declined so shockingly in the U.S. It is society as a whole—what I term the "un-culture." America has become a nation of obese, dumbed-down television addicts, who live vicariously through a galaxy of the most vapid, self-absorbed "stars."

The average person spends an enormous amount of their time fixated on their smartphone. They sit on a bus texting their 347 cyber "friends" while being unable to make a new, real friend in the seat beside them—because that person is buried in their iPhone.

The movie industry, which both shapes and reflects the public consciousness, can no longer make a film about the complex joys and sorrows of actual people. Instead, they spew out preposterous comic book superhero fantasies that grotesquely distort the true human condition. This produces a population of dangerous male adults with violent juvenile values.

To highlight how sad and ludicrous daily existence in the USA has become, here are some of the categories in which America either leads the world or is near the top:

- Obesity
- Out-of-wedlock teen pregnancy
- Incarcerated citizens
- Laws, rules and regulations
- Mentally ill people
- Consumption of illegal drugs
- Fast food consumption
- Rapes, including those in prisons
- Military spending
- TV viewing by school-age children
- Prescription drug use
- Arms sales to foreign countries
- Broken families and children born into poverty
- Indebtedness

Hopefully, you are a lot less inclined to chant "We're #1" or "U-S-A" after seeing that list. Although I referred to it jokingly as Insaneistan, it should be clear from my synopsis that the situation in the USA is not funny at all. It used to be wonderful in so many ways, but now it has deteriorated so profoundly that it is just a sad, tragic caricature of its former greatness.

* * *

It's twilight now, and I've added a touch of rum to my Tarzan Tea. I chuckle while pondering whether this is to avoid melancholy or to embrace it. A black-crowned night heron glides by,

140

and the kind words of my friends revisit me. "I mean, come on, Ray, this sea gypsy stuff is fine for a while, but isn't it time that you came home?" Fortunately, *I Am Home!* And even though my neighbors may be dolphins and egrets and spotted eagle rays, our world is sweet and genuine and enduring.

The Useless Joy of Juggling

*T*UCKED AWAY in the backwaters of these essays, there are a few brief references to a prior chapter in my life when I was a... *Juggler*. And as might be expected, due to my fondness for the Unconventional Path, I did not juggle in ordinary venues like circuses or Las Vegas revues. No, I was a street performer—and proud of it. Indeed, I am *still* proud of it—because I was the very first of the San Francisco street jugglers.

This was back in the early 1970s, when street performing was beginning its modern American renaissance. Those were glorious years, when the sidewalks were alive with mimes and tap dancers and magicians and roller-skating accordionists. Because we were pioneers, we were all joyously making it up as we went along. As a continuation of the Sixties' mentality of "let's really embrace life," our ragtag band of buskers was predominantly motivated by cooperation rather than competition. We preferred being folk heroes to being stars. As an unrepentant romantic, this was an exquisite community for me. I could live frugally but comfortably, while making my favorite city a slightly better and happier place. And my modest efforts were respected and cherished by my neighbors. The Mayor of San Francisco even declared a day in my honor.

That wistful-golden era lasted about two decades and then it began to tarnish. Being a beloved San Francisco street enter-tainer was no longer enough for the newer performers. They wanted to use the streets as a stepping stone to comedy clubs and sitcoms and "the big time." Witnessing this decline was too heartbreaking for me, and so I sailed away from it all—and began my sea gypsy life.

* * *

I do not regret that decision, but every once in a while the strange enchantment of juggling seduces me again. It has done so recently; and since my natural inclination is to examine my impulses, I have tried to determine why this eccentric skill re-mains so alluring to me. After pondering this for a few days, it became apparent that there are some larger life lessons inher-ent in this unusual talent that might be worth sharing with you, my unknown irregulars.

I began writing these essays 19 months ago, and since then my life has become exceedingly cerebral—too much emphasis on my mental faculties and not enough on my physical capaci-ties. I do rigorously exercise almost every day, but still the ra-tio of thinking to moving has gotten way out of balance.

So after a few years of neglect, I decided to see how my jug-gling skills were holding up. I feared that since I am now in my middle years there would be a severe decline in my ability. What a welcome surprise it has been to discover that I can still do my most difficult moves, such as five balls and torches blindfolded and the bowling balls. Even more delightful has been the realization that I can also learn new tricks that I had never attempted previously.

But aside from my enjoyment of reconnecting with an old skill and passion, I have also gained a deeper awareness of the less-appreciated aspects of this unusual art form. This fresh evaluation of the merits of juggling has convinced me that it would be an ideal semi-athletic activity for my Sea Gypsy Tribe. Here are some of the reasons for this conclusion:

- **Universality.** It is universal in two main ways. First, the basic skill can be mastered by almost anyone. When I used to get hired to teach juggling at grammar schools, the child who could not learn was a genuine rarity. It is accessible to almost everyone blessed with basic human coordination. And this goes for elders as well as youngsters. I have successfully taught many people who swore that they were "too old to learn." In a world that tries to convince older people that their physical capabilities have vanished, the silly little art of juggling is proof that this does not have to be so.
- **Universality 2.0.** Its other universality is its appeal. Young or old, rich or poor, vegan or carnivore—almost everyone enjoys the dancing objects that a master juggler can control. I proved this in 1979-80 when I juggled my way around the world, paying for my travels by doing my show and passing my hat in a hundred exotic locales.
- **Inexpensive.** It is one of the cheapest quasi-sports that exist. Basic rubber balls cost only a few dollars and even professional quality props only involve an expenditure of a few hundred dollars.
- **Useless.** In a world where everything must have some commercial value, recreational juggling is an abysmal yet delightful failure. The well-worn parental warning of "Yes, that's a nice hobby, but what can you *do* with it?" rings profoundly true. I would doubt that one of every thousand people who learn how to juggle is able to earn a living from it. That is a big part of its oddball charm—it is not utilitarian—it is joyous!
- **Better Than Meditation.** As someone who is mostly from San Francisco, I dutifully tried meditation a few times in my life. What I discovered was that juggling is far more Zen than sitting on a mat attempting to clear my mind and not think of a bear riding a bicycle. The concept of "no mind" is perfectly

activated by juggling. If one concentrates too intensely on the escaping objects then you tense up and they elude you. And if you don't focus enough on the manipulation, you also fail. So there is an ideal "zone" that you must enter in order to "be here now" simultaneous to your objects also being "present."

• **Simplicity.** In an entertainment world dominated by high-tech electro-spectacles, a single individual with three cascading spheres can still mesmerize a crowd—be they Parisian sophisticates or Chinese tea plantation workers. I know this definitively.

• **Attainable Joy.** When a new student gets the knack and can actually keep the balls flying for as long as they wish, a flood of delight sweeps over them. And then with each new trick that they master, a similar rush of achievement and excitement flows through them. Another great aspect is that there are innumerable juggling patterns that involve groups of people passing objects back and forth. So there is a lot of emphasis on cooperation and the success of the clan.

• **It Is Not Effortless.** Another great aspect of learning to juggle is that it takes genuine *effort*. There are no easy shortcuts. You must fail a thousand times, reach down and pick up the object and try again until you learn it. In a world where so many people want everything handed to them, this is a skill that must actually be earned.

• **Electrically Independent.** If the grid goes down the fun still continues.

• **It Allows Elegant Artistry.** Street juggling relies heavily on humorous banter with the audience. However, in recent years a new type has emerged that I call "artistic juggling." This combines the manipulation of objects with music and movement. The emergence of Cirque de Soleil did much to promote this distinctive and captivating style. So now there are many jugglers whose routines are dance-like and almost hypnotic.

Now that I have described the many wondrous attributes of juggling that are not obvious to most people, you can probably understand why I wish to make it a signature element in my Sea Gypsy Tribe. It will be a superb way to deepen the bonds between the tribal members, and since it is not age-specific, it can be enjoyed by both the pre-teens and the elders.

* * *

I believe that if there is an enormous global collapse (and as always, I hope that I am wrong!) that various Sea Gypsy Tribes scattered about the planet have an excellent chance of surviv- ing the devastation. My guess is that after a prolonged period at sea the sailboats will return to the shore and find some abandoned spot that will provide a suitable land base for a new community. They will plant the vegetable seeds that they have been carrying, build shelters and secure the perimeter. A group will be left there to raise the children and tend the crops and the chickens.

But for at least the first few years, there will also need to be periods when the ships return to the sea on exploration and salvage voyages, trying to find out who else made it through, and seeking gear and tools that might be valuable to the colony ashore.

Each time the fleet returns safely from their expedition, I envision a welcome home ceremony with the entire village gathered on the headland juggling balls and clubs and torches to welcome home the weary mariners. It is a joyous vision.

Catastrophic Progress

*T*HE DEEP SERENITY down here in the Archipelago of Bliss soothes and inspires me. Sometimes *Aventura* and I find a tiny lagoon that is so tranquil that the silence almost seems to speak. In many spots the jungle runs all the way down to the sea. Such symbolism comforts me, be - cause they are both such essential incubators of life.

Last week I found a bay so sublime that the voice of nature was louder than the clamor of humanity. On a typical day I would see 25 dugout cayucos being quietly rowed by extremely fit Indios. Only rarely was the stillness disturbed by a boat with an engine. Most of the human sounds came from happy children—laughing and playing in the shallow water.

A little cabin on the shore caught my eye. It seemed like a perfect hideaway for a writer, and I imagined Thoreau sitting on its tiny porch in the twilight savoring a day well-spent on reflecting and writing. I believe that if he lived today he would choose a sailing boat as his platform for observing and commenting on Life. A cabin on Walden Pond would be impossibly expensive, and he would chafe at the preposterous restrictions that the bureaucrats would demand.

I have long felt that he too would choose the Sea Gypsy Philosopher life. This intuition was recently reinforced for me when I learned that the final sentence that he uttered on his deathbed was, "Now comes good sailing!" These thoughts led to a deeper meditation on how astonishingly different the world is now—in just the 153 years since his death.

* * *

Here are some of the universal themes that dominated Henry David Thoreau's thinking and writing:

• The need for people to stay connected to and reverent towards Nature. Otherwise, they will suffer great psychic damage as both individuals and as societies.
• The importance of recognizing that the Individual should be more powerful than the State—and that the best governments are those that govern the *least!*
• The urgent need to fight against injustice, whether it came in the form of slavery or tyrannical imperialism.
• The value of simple living as a way of avoiding the distractions of the modern world and thus discovering life's deeper meaning.

Even though Thoreau provided wise and prophetic counsel on these topics, his guidance was largely ignored. Let's assess how humanity has dealt with these issues in the century and a half since he died.

• **Reverence For Nature.** The human-built world has become so dominant that for most people an experience of Nature means a vacation in a national park, a preserve that is like a theme park except that it is filled with trees and bears and geysers. Even agriculture is barely natural anymore. The soil is gone and replaced with a thin veneer of fertilizers and pesticides and herbicides. And the farmers spend most of their time driving enormous air-conditioned tractors and combines.

• **Power To The People.** The brilliant and noble concept of government "by, for and of the people" has been so distorted that it is a mockery of the original intention of the Founding Fathers. And this is not just in the U.S., for almost all nations now have "elected representatives" who are just puppets for the tiny rich elites who really pull the strings of power.

• **Battling Injustice.** Those who wield the levers of power continue to shape a world which is dominated by a few rulers and an enormous mass of people who are ruled. Unfortunately, these people are as clever as they are ruthless. So instead of shaking an iron fist, they wield their control more subtly—using meaningless elections and a lapdog media.

• **Simplicity or Clarity.** The modern world is a tsunami of electronic gadgetry that is drowning humanity with tiny machines that complicate our lives instead of simplifying them. People spend their days staring at screens that are LCD replacements for authentic living.

So what would Thoreau think about this "progress" that we have achieved in the last century and a half? Presumably, he would be appalled and outraged. But these issues that he was crusading against are actually puny when compared with the problems that humanity faces today. That's because in those days we had the technology to harm one another, but we didn't yet have the means to actually exterminate the entire human project. But in one of his lesser-known quotations Thoreau does allude to man's horrible capacity for malice and destruction: "Thank god men cannot fly, and lay waste the sky as well as the earth."

But in fact, we have "laid waste" to the sky and the earth and the sea. And we are faced with such enormous problems that the very existence of humankind is at risk. Fortunately, if we do manage to drive ourselves to extinction, our small, wet, lush planet will survive. And eventually Mother Earth will heal the wounds that 10,000 years of human civilization—and especially 300 years of industrial advancement—have heaped upon her.

I realize that this seems like blasphemy, since we are bombarded with messaging that assures us that the rise of capital-C Civilization is the best thing that ever happened to the planet. But a visionary like Thoreau would clearly recognize that we are defiling and destroying our one and only support system. The lunacy would be obvious to him. And to those who might not perceive it, let me mention a few possible ways that we may very well end our stay on the planet in the very near future.

• **Climate Chaos.** Despite the efforts of the rich and immoral industrialists bankrolling the climate change denial camp, the mass of evidence from "un-bought" scientists is overwhelming. Our human conduct is profoundly altering the very biological, geological and atmospheric functioning of the planet. And those who think that the looming disasters will be gradual and manageable have not examined the ice and tree core data that clearly shows catastrophic climate change often occurs swiftly and violently.

• **Nuclear Insanity.** The movement by the most hawkish and psychotic elements of the U.S. political and military "leadership" to reignite the Cold War should be terrifying to everyone. And yet it is barely noticed by the general population, who are largely fixated on their iDistractors. Instead of the long-standing policy of only launching nuclear missiles if fired upon by an enemy, a new "first-strike" policy has been quietly installed by the U.S. Plus, money is now being allocated by multiple governments for new generations of even-more-lethal nuclear weapons. And with the rise of computer hacking, the dangers become multiplied even more ominously.

• **Worldwide Pandemic.** This risk has several variations. A superbug could spread rapidly around the world because of how interconnected the planet now is through air travel and long-distance food shipping. Or more maliciously, evil elements—be they terrorists or tyrannical governments—could release some of the many horrific bio-weapons that have been developed in recent decades. Or such a weapon could escape accidentally through an explosion in a lab where such hideous concoctions are developed.

• **Nuclear Power Disasters.** Let me count the ways... earthquakes, tsunamis, grid-down power outages stopping the cooling pond pumps, sabotage, human error by technicians, spent fuel rods with no place to go. What could possibly go wrong?

• **Transhumanism and Robot Rebellion.** The plot lines of B-grade science fiction movies are rapidly becoming possible realities. The maniacs who refuse to embrace and abide by the laws of nature have now conjured up these new threats to human survival. Why do they do it? For human and planetary betterment—or for fame and fortune? You be the judge.

* * *

And so as I sit here in this stunningly peaceful lagoon staring at the little Walden cabin by the sea, I am deeply saddened by the disastrous evolution of the human project since the days of Thoreau. If he were alive today he would undoubtedly speak more insightfully and convincingly than I can on these profound subjects. But my hope is that I can capture a bit of his phantom spirit ghosting about in that tiny cabin—and use it to give my own words more power and eloquence.

19995252R00100

Made in the USA
Middletown, DE
11 May 2015